Of Synthetic Finance

Synthetic finance revolutionizes materialism such that we can now create wealth in the process of universally distributing it. While financial innovation in global capitalism provided the conditions for the 2008 financial crisis, it has also engineered a set of financial technologies with universal distributive potential. This book explains this possibility and demonstrates how it can be achieved through a rigorous ontological exposition of the radical, nomadic, distributive power of synthetic finance. It also illustrates that Gilles Deleuze is the heterodox political economist who best reveals its profound material capacities.

This book articulates an innovative method for the study of finance, fundamentally re-evaluates political economy as a discipline and practice, and inaugurates a research project from which derivative methodologies and approaches to critical finance can evolve. *Of Synthetic Finance* actualizes a new kind of heterodox political economy called speculative materialism, and advocates a radical project of speculative materialist financial engineering. Both of these are predicated on the deployment of the latent, nomadic, monstrous capacities of synthetic finance to create and universally distribute risk and cash flow.

This book is a must read for anyone interested in critical finance, the financial crisis and the future of political economy.

Benjamin Lozano is Instructor, Curriculum Coordinator and Researcher at The Bruce Initiative on Rethinking Capitalism, UC Santa Cruz, USA.

Routledge Frontiers of Political Economy

1 **Equilibrium Versus Understanding**
Towards the rehumanization of economics within social theory
Mark Addleson

2 **Evolution, Order and Complexity**
Edited by Elias L. Khalil and Kenneth E. Boulding

3 **Interactions in Political Economy**
Malvern after ten years
Edited by Steven Pressman

4 **The End of Economics**
Michael Perelman

5 **Probability in Economics**
Omar F. Hamouda and Robin Rowley

6 **Capital Controversy, Post Keynesian Economics and the History of Economics**
Essays in honour of Geoff Harcourt, volume one
Edited by Philip Arestis, Gabriel Palma and Malcolm Sawyer

7 **Markets, Unemployment and Economic Policy**
Essays in honour of Geoff Harcourt, volume two
Edited by Philip Arestis, Gabriel Palma and Malcolm Sawyer

8 **Social Economy**
The logic of capitalist development
Clark Everling

9 **New Keynesian Economics/Post Keynesian Alternatives**
Edited by Roy J. Rotheim

10 **The Representative Agent in Macroeconomics**
James E. Hartley

11 **Borderlands of Economics**
Essays in honour of Daniel R. Fusfeld
Edited by Nahid Aslanbeigui and Young Back Choi

12 **Value, Distribution and Capital**
Essays in honour of Pierangelo Garegnani
Edited by Gary Mongiovi and Fabio Petri

13 **The Economics of Science**
Methodology and epistemology as if economics really mattered
James R. Wible

14 **Competitiveness, Localised Learning and Regional Development**
Specialisation and prosperity in small open economies
Peter Maskell, Heikki Eskelinen, Ingjaldur Hannibalsson, Anders Malmberg and Eirik Vatne

15 **Labour Market Theory**
A constructive reassessment
Ben J. Fine

16 **Women and European Employment**
Jill Rubery, Mark Smith, Colette Fagan and Damian Grimshaw

17 **Explorations in Economic Methodology**
From Lakatos to empirical philosophy of science
Roger Backhouse

18 **Subjectivity in Political Economy**
Essays on wanting and choosing
David P. Levine

19 **The Political Economy of Middle East Peace**
The impact of competing trade agendas
Edited by J.W. Wright, Jnr

20 **The Active Consumer**
Novelty and surprise in consumer choice
Edited by Marina Bianchi

21 **Subjectivism and Economic Analysis**
Essays in memory of Ludwig Lachmann
Edited by Roger Koppl and Gary Mongiovi

22 **Themes in Post-Keynesian Economics**
Essays in honour of Geoff Harcourt, volume three
Edited by Claudio Sardoni and Peter Kriesler

23 **The Dynamics of Technological Knowledge**
Cristiano Antonelli

24 **The Political Economy of Diet, Health and Food Policy**
Ben J. Fine

25 **The End of Finance**
Capital market inflation, financial derivatives and pension fund capitalism
Jan Toporowski

26 **Political Economy and the New Capitalism**
Edited by Jan Toporowski

27 **Growth Theory**
A philosophical perspective
Patricia Northover

28 **The Political Economy of the Small Firm**
Charles Dannreuther and Lew Perren

29 **Hahn and Economic Methodology**
Edited by Thomas Boylan and Paschal F. O'Gorman

30 **Gender, Growth and Trade**
The miracle economies of the postwar years
David Kucera

31 **Normative Political Economy**
Subjective freedom, the market and the state
David Levine

32 **Economist with a Public Purpose**
Essays in honour of John Kenneth Galbraith
Edited by Michael Keaney

33 **Involuntary Unemployment**
The elusive quest for a theory
Michel De Vroey

34 **The Fundamental Institutions of Capitalism**
Ernesto Screpanti

35 **Transcending Transaction**
The search for self-generating markets
Alan Shipman

36 **Power in Business and the State**
An historical analysis of its concentration
Frank Bealey

37 **Editing Economics**
Essays in honour of Mark Perlman
Hank Lim, Ungsuh K. Park and Geoff Harcourt

38 **Money, Macroeconomics and Keynes**
Essays in honour of Victoria Chick, volume I
Philip Arestis, Meghnad Desai and Sheila Dow

39 **Methodology, Microeconomics and Keynes**
Essays in honour of Victoria Chick, volume II
Philip Arestis, Meghnad Desai and Sheila Dow

40 **Market Drive and Governance**
Reexamining the rules for economic and commercial contest
Ralf Boscheck

41 **The Value of Marx**
Political economy for contemporary capitalism
Alfredo Saad-Filho

42 **Issues in Positive Political Economy**
S. Mansoob Murshed

43 **The Enigma of Globalisation**
A journey to a new stage of capitalism
Robert Went

44 **The Market**
Equilibrium, stability, mythology
S.N. Afriat

45 **The Political Economy of Rule Evasion and Policy Reform**
Jim Leitzel

46 **Unpaid Work and the Economy**
Edited by Antonella Picchio

47 **Distributional Justice**
Theory and measurement
Hilde Bojer

48 **Cognitive Developments in Economics**
Edited by Salvatore Rizzello

49 **Social Foundations of Markets, Money and Credit**
Costas Lapavitsas

50 **Rethinking Capitalist Development**
Essays on the economics of Josef Steindl
Edited by Tracy Mott and Nina Shapiro

51 **An Evolutionary Approach to Social Welfare**
Christian Sartorius

52 **Kalecki's Economics Today**
Edited by Zdzislaw L. Sadowski and Adam Szeworski

53 **Fiscal Policy from Reagan to Blair**
The left veers right
Ravi K. Roy and Arthur T. Denzau

54 **The Cognitive Mechanics of Economic Development and Institutional Change**
Bertin Martens

55 **Individualism and the Social Order**
The social element in liberal thought
Charles R. McCann Jnr.

56 **Affirmative Action in the United States and India**
A comparative perspective
Thomas E. Weisskopf

57 **Global Political Economy and the Wealth of Nations**
Performance, institutions, problems and policies
Edited by Phillip Anthony O'Hara

58 **Structural Economics**
Thijs ten Raa

59 **Macroeconomic Theory and Economic Policy**
Essays in honour of Jean-Paul Fitoussi
Edited by K. Vela Velupillai

60 **The Struggle Over Work**
The "end of work" and employment alternatives in post-industrial societies
Shaun Wilson

61 **The Political Economy of Global Sporting Organisations**
John Forster and Nigel Pope

62 **The Flawed Foundations of General Equilibrium Theory**
Critical essays on economic theory
Frank Ackerman and Alejandro Nadal

63 **Uncertainty in Economic Theory**
Essays in honour of David Schmeidler's 65th birthday
Edited by Itzhak Gilboa

64 **The New Institutional Economics of Corruption**
Edited by Johann Graf Lambsdorff, Markus Taube and Matthias Schramm

65 **The Price Index and its Extension**
A chapter in economic measurement
S.N. Afriat

66 **Reduction, Rationality and Game Theory in Marxian Economics**
Bruce Philp

67 **Culture and Politics in Economic Development**
Volker Bornschier

68 **Modern Applications of Austrian Thought**
Edited by Jürgen G. Backhaus

69 **Ordinary Choices**
Individuals, incommensurability, and democracy
Robert Urquhart

70 **Labour Theory of Value**
Peter C. Dooley

71 **Capitalism**
Victor D. Lippit

72 **Macroeconomic Foundations of Macroeconomics**
Alvaro Cencini

73 **Marx for the 21st Century**
Edited by Hiroshi Uchida

74 **Growth and Development in the Global Political Economy**
Social structures of accumulation and modes of regulation
Phillip Anthony O'Hara

75 **The New Economy and Macroeconomic Stability**
A neo-modern perspective drawing on the complexity approach and Keynesian economics
Teodoro Dario Togati

76 **The Future of Social Security Policy**
Women, work and a citizens basic income
Ailsa McKay

77 **Clinton and Blair**
The political economy of the Third Way
Flavio Romano

78 **Marxian Reproduction Schema**
Money and aggregate demand in a capitalist economy
A.B. Trigg

79 **The Core Theory in Economics**
Problems and solutions
Lester G. Telser

80 **Economics, Ethics and the Market**
Introduction and applications
Johan J. Graafland

81 **Social Costs and Public Action in Modern Capitalism**
Essays inspired by Karl William Kapp's Theory of Social Costs
Edited by Wolfram Elsner, Pietro Frigato and Paolo Ramazzotti

82 **Globalization and the Myths of Free Trade**
History, theory and empirical evidence
Edited by Anwar Shaikh

83 **Equilibrium in Economics**
Scope and Limits
Edited by Valeria Mosini

84 **Globalization**
State of the art and perspectives
Edited by Stefan A. Schirm

85 **Neoliberalism**
National and regional experiments with global ideas
Edited by Ravi K. Roy, Arthur T. Denzau and Thomas D. Willett

86 **Post-Keynesian Macroeconomics Economics**
Essays in honour of Ingrid Rima
Edited by Mathew Forstater, Gary Mongiovi and Steven Pressman

87 **Consumer Capitalism**
Anastasios S. Korkotsides

88 **Remapping Gender in the New Global Order**
Edited by Marjorie Griffin Cohen and Janine Brodie

89 **Hayek and Natural Law**
Erik Angner

90 **Race and Economic Opportunity in the Twenty-First Century**
Edited by Marlene Kim

91 **Renaissance in Behavioural Economics**
Harvey Leibenstein's impact on contemporary economic analysis
Edited by Roger Frantz

92 **Human Ecology Economics**
A new framework for global sustainability
Edited by Roy E. Allen

93 **Imagining Economics Otherwise**
Encounters with identity/difference
Nitasha Kaul

94 **Reigniting the Labor Movement**
Restoring means to ends in a democratic labor movement
Gerald Friedman

95 **The Spatial Model of Politics**
Norman Schofield

96 **The Economics of American Judaism**
Carmel Ullman Chiswick

97 **Critical Political Economy**
Christian Arnsperger

98 **Culture and Economic Explanation**
Economics in the US and Japan
Donald W. Katzner

99 **Feminism, Economics and Utopia**
Time travelling through paradigms
Karin Schönpflug

100 **Risk in International Finance**
Vikash Yadav

101 **Economic Policy and Performance in Industrial Democracies**
Party governments, central banks and the fiscal–monetary policy mix
Takayuki Sakamoto

102 **Advances on Income Inequality and Concentration Measures**
Edited by Gianni Betti and Achille Lemmi

103 **Economic Representations**
Academic and everyday
Edited by David F. Ruccio

104 **Mathematical Economics and the Dynamics of Capitalism**
Goodwin's legacy continued
Edited by Peter Flaschel and Michael Landesmann

105 **The Keynesian Multiplier**
Edited by Claude Gnos and Louis-Philippe Rochon

106 **Money, Enterprise and Income Distribution**
Towards a macroeconomic theory of capitalism
John Smithin

107 Fiscal Decentralization and Local Public Finance in Japan
Nobuki Mochida

108 The 'Uncertain' Foundations of Post-Keynesian Economics
Essays in exploration
Stephen P. Dunn

109 Karl Marx's Grundrisse
Foundations of the critique of political economy 150 years later
Edited by Marcello Musto

110 Economics and the Price Index
S.N. Afriat and Carlo Milana

111 Sublime Economy
On the intersection of art and economics
Edited by Jack Amariglio, Joseph W. Childers and Stephen E. Cullenberg

112 Popper, Hayek and the Open Society
Calvin Hayes

113 The Political Economy of Work
David Spencer

114 Institutional Economics
Bernard Chavance

115 Religion, Economics and Demography
The effects of religion on education, work, and the family
Evelyn L. Lehrer

116 Economics, Rational Choice and Normative Philosophy
Edited by Thomas A. Boylan and Ruvin Gekker

117 Economics Versus Human Rights
Manuel Couret Branco

118 Hayek Versus Marx and Today's Challenges
Eric Aarons

119 Work Time Regulation as Sustainable Full Employment Policy
Robert LaJeunesse

120 Equilibrium, Welfare and Uncertainty
Mukul Majumdar

121 Capitalism, Institutions and Economic Development
Michael Heller

122 Economic Pluralism
Robert Garnett, Erik Olsen and Martha Starr

123 Dialectics of Class Struggle in the Global Economy
Clark Everling

124 Political Economy and Globalization
Richard Westra

125 Full-Spectrum Economics
Toward an inclusive and emancipatory social science
Christian Arnsperger

126 Computable, Constructive and Behavioural Economic Dynamics
Essays in honour of Kumaraswamy (Vela) Velupillai
Stefano Zambelli

127 **Monetary Macrodynamics**
Toichiro Asada, Carl Chiarella, Peter Flaschel and Reiner Franke

128 **Rationality and Explanation in Economics**
Maurice Lagueux

129 **The Market, Happiness and Solidarity**
A Christian perspective
Johan J. Graafland

130 **Economic Complexity and Equilibrium Illusion**
Essays on market instability and macro vitality
Ping Chen

131 **Economic Theory and Social Change**
Problems and revisions
Hasse Ekstedt and Angelo Fusari

132 **The Practices of Happiness**
Political economy, religion and wellbeing
Edited by John Atherton, Elaine Graham and Ian Steedman

133 **The Measurement of Individual Well-Being and Group Inequalities**
Essays in memory of Z.M. Berrebi
Edited by Joseph Deutsch and Jacques Silber

134 **Wage Policy, Income Distribution, and Democratic Theory**
Oren M. Levin-Waldman

135 **The Political Economy of Bureaucracy**
Steven O. Richardson

136 **The Moral Rhetoric of Political Economy**
Justice and modern economic thought
Paul Turpin

137 **Macroeconomic Regimes in Western Industrial Countries**
Hansjörg Herr and Milka Kazandziska

138 **Business Ethics and the Austrian Tradition in Economics**
Hardy Bouillon

139 **Inequality and Power**
The economics of class
Eric A. Schutz

140 **Capital as a Social Kind**
Definitions and transformations in the critique of political economy
Howard Engelskirchen

141 **Happiness, Ethics and Economics**
Johannes Hirata

142 **Capital, Exploitation and Economic Crisis**
John Weeks

143 **The Global Economic Crisis**
New perspectives on the critique of economic theory and policy
Edited by Emiliano Brancaccio and Giuseppe Fontana

144 **Economics and Diversity**
Carlo D'Ippoliti

145 **Political Economy of Human Rights**
Rights, realities and realization
Bas de Gaay Fortman

146 Robinson Crusoe's Economic Man
A construction and deconstruction
Edited by Ulla Grapard and Gillian Hewitson

147 Freedom and Happiness in Economic Thought and Philosophy
From clash to reconciliation
Edited by Ragip Ege and Herrade Igersheim

148 Political Economy After Economics
David Laibman

149 Reconstructing Keynesian Macroeconomics, Volume 1
Partial perspectives
Carl Chiarella, Peter Flaschel and Willi Semmler

150 Institutional Economics and National Competitiveness
Edited by Young Back Choi

151 Capitalist Diversity and Diversity within Capitalism
Edited by Geoffrey T. Wood and Christel Lane

152 The Consumer, Credit and Neoliberalism
Governing the modern economy
Christopher Payne

153 Order and Control in American Socio-Economic Thought
U.S. social scientists and progressive-era reform
Charles McCann

154 The Irreconcilable Inconsistencies of Neoclassical Macroeconomics
A false paradigm
John Weeks

155 The Political Economy of Putin's Russia
Pekka Sutela

156 Facts, Values and Objectivity in Economics
José Castro Caldas and Vítor Neves

157 Economic Growth and the High Wage Economy
Choices, constraints and opportunities in the market economy
Morris Altman

158 Social Costs Today
Institutional analyses of the present crises
Edited by Wolfram Elsner, Pietro Frigato and Paolo Ramazzotti

159 Economics, Sustainability and Democracy
Economics in the era of climate change
Christopher Nobbs

160 Organizations, Individualism and Economic Theory
Maria Brouwer

161 Economic Models for Policy Making
Principles and designs revisited
S.I. Cohen

162 Reconstructing Keynesian Macroeconomics, Volume 2
Integrated approaches
Carl Chiarella, Peter Flaschel and Willi Semmler

163 Architectures of Economic Subjectivity
The philosophical foundations of the subject in the history of economic thought
Sonya Marie Scott

164 Support-Bargaining, Economics and Society
A social species
Patrick Spread

165 Inherited Wealth, Justice and Equality
Edited by Guido Erreygers and John Cunliffe

166 The Charismatic Principle in Social Life
Edited by Luigino Bruni and Barbara Sena

167 Ownership Economics
On the foundations of interest, money, markets, business cycles and economic development
Gunnar Heinsohn and Otto Steiger; translated and edited with comments and additions by Frank Decker

168 Urban and Regional Development Trajectories in Contemporary Capitalism
Edited by Flavia Martinelli, Frank Moulaert and Andreas Novy

169 Social Fairness and Economics
Economic essays in the spirit of Duncan Foley
Edited by Lance Taylor, Armon Rezai and Thomas Michl

170 Financial Crisis, Labour Markets and Institutions
Edited by Sebastiano Fadda and Pasquale Tridico

171 Marx and Living Labour
Laurent Baronian

172 A Political Economy of Contemporary Capitalism and its Crisis
Demystifying finance
Dimitris P. Sotiropoulos, John G. Milios and Spyros Lapatsioras

173 Against Utility-Based Economics
On a life-based approach
Anastasios Korkotsides

174 Economic Indeterminacy
The dance of the meta-axioms
Yanis Varoufakis

175 Freedom, Responsibility and Economics of the Person
Jérôme Ballet, Damien Bazin, Jean-Luc Dubois and François-Régis Mahieu

176 Reality and Accounting
Ontological explorations in the economic and social sciences
Richard Mattessich

177 Profitability and the Great Recession
The role of accumulation trends in the financial crisis
Ascension Mejorado and Manuel Roman

178 **Institutions and Development After the Financial Crisis**
Edited by Sebastiano Fadda and Pasquale Tridico

179 **The Political Economy of Gunnar Myrdal**
A reassessment in the post-2008 world
Örjan Appelqvist

180 **Gender Perspectives and Gender Impacts of the Global Economic Crisis**
Edited by Rania Antonopoulos

181 **Hegel, Institutions, and Economics**
Performing the social
Carsten Herrmann-Pillath and Ivan A. Boldyrev

182 **Producer Cooperatives as a New Mode of Production**
Bruno Jossa

183 **Economic Policy and the Financial Crisis**
Edited by Łukasz Mamica and Pasquale Tridico

184 **Information Technology and Socialist Construction**
The end of capital and the transition to socialism
Daniel E. Saros

185 **Beyond Mainstream Explanations of the Financial Crisis**
Parasitic finance capital
Ismael Hossein-zadeh

186 **Greek Capitalism in Crisis**
Marxist analyses
Stavros Mavroudeas

187 **Of Synthetic Finance**
Three essays of speculative materialism
Benjamin Lozano

188 **The Political Economy and Media Coverage of the European Economic Crisis**
The case of Ireland
Julien Mercille

Of Synthetic Finance

Three essays of speculative materialism

Benjamin Lozano

Routledge
Taylor & Francis Group
LONDON AND NEW YORK

First published 2015 by Routledge

2 Park Square, Milton Park, Abingdon, Oxfordshire OX14 4RN
711 Third Avenue, New York, NY 10017

Routledge is an imprint of the Taylor & Francis Group, an informa business

First issued in paperback 2018

British Library Cataloguing in Publication Data
A catalogue record for this book is available from the British Library

Library of Congress Cataloging in Publication Data
Lozano, Benjamin.
Of synthetic finance: three essays of speculative materialism / Benjamin Lozano.
pages cm – (Routledge frontiers of political economy)
Includes bibliographical references and index.
1. Finance. 2. Capitalism. I. Title.
HG173.L696 2014
332.01–dc23 2014005955

ISBN: 978-1-138-79084-1 (hbk)
ISBN: 978-1-138-37932-9 (pbk)

Typeset in Times New Roman
by Wearset Ltd, Boldon, Tyne and Wear

For Kate, Channing, and Serra
Proof of singularity, and difference in repetition

Contents

Illustrations

Figures

Table

Acknowledgments

I am indebted to different formal and informal interlocutors – those still hoisting backpacks, those wearing cotton sweaters and tweed jackets, those donning business suits – who stand on varieties of plateaus in their intellectual development, politics and philosophical commitments. Special mention is given to Bob Meister and Steve Bruce of The Bruce Initiative on Rethinking Capitalism out of UC Santa Cruz, without whose vision, original notions and gracious support any project inaugurated by this book would yet remain latent. Also, Randy Martin and the rest of The Cultures of Finance working group out of NYU are acknowledged for effecting a propulsive clearing in the woods for thinking critically – not just at or about – but *with* finance. I am grateful for and honored by our affiliation.

Figures for Essays One and Two were designed by Natalie Brescia, and Figures for the Appendices were designed by Maren Slobody. Both of these artists' refined communicative intuition and acute aesthetic sensibility were indispensable to the necessary task of retranslating some of this book's core concepts into visual images.

Introduction

i. When directing our attention to the properties of financial assets, it is striking to encounter an ontological domain both peculiar and rich with consequences for our understanding of materiality.

Nobel Prize-winning economist, James Tobin, held a passing interest in such properties – though his approach, perhaps unsurprisingly, lacks adequate appreciation of the ontological domain to which we are directed. In his essay titled 'Properties of Assets' Tobin sets out to analyze 'the fundamental properties of assets,' which he asserts are (a) 'determined by their intrinsic natures' and (b) determined by 'the markets in which they are traded.'[1]

Let us bracket any critique of the essentialism infecting Tobin's premise that properties of financial assets are 'intrinsic' to their 'nature' – as if economic objects were Platonic figures, whose properties are primary, natural, or inherent to some self-enclosed, fixed, Euclidean space – in order to concern ourselves with the more promising features of his pursuit. It is instructive to reflect on Tobin's inaugural self-conscious attempt to identify 'the fundamental properties of assets' in light of subsequent approaches to this task; and to then glean from these approaches the necessary resources to calibrate our own inaugural attempt to study the ontology of finance.

We begin by asking a first question: What are some properties of financial assets?

Tobin, writing in the early 1960s, non-exhaustively classifies six 'fundamental properties': *liquidity*, *reversibility*, *divisibility*, *predictability*, and *yield and return.* Forty years later Fabozzi, Modigliani, and Jones, in their textbook *Foundations of Financial Markets and Institutions* (1st ed. 2002, 4th ed. 2009), resume Tobin's exercise by expanding his list to eleven properties: *moneyness*, *divisibility*, *reversibility*, *cash flow*, *term to maturity*, *convertibility*, *currency*, *liquidity*, *return predictability*, *complexity*, and *tax status*. More recently Allan Malz, in his *Financial Risk Management: Models, History, and Institutions* (2011), while also providing no definitive list, is writing after the 2007–2008 financial crisis, and so now discusses all aforementioned properties under the general illumination of the *über*-property of *risk* – today, that property which, for Malz, bathes all other colors of economic properties and modifies their particularity.

We use these approaches as base elements from which to build our own list of properties; and yet we are far too impatient to attempt a comprehensive recovery of the entirety of Tobin's analysis, the expanded catalog provided by Fabozzi *et al.*, or the risk-as-structuring-principle approach of Malz. Rather, to begin we are interested in the ontological implications of their treatments of the properties of assets, and find them useful as a preliminary step to reflecting on the unique and peculiar but profound and potentially radical material properties of synthetic finance.

ii. Our attention is also drawn to the second half of Tobin's objective – namely, to study the 'properties of assets, *as determined by…the markets in which they are traded.*'

We will excuse our reader for initially regarding as unremarkable the premise embedded herein. A common belief surreptitiously imported into Tobin's this-time warranted presumption is that to proceed with an analysis of the properties of financial assets, we are in turn required to examine the market qua space of exchange in which the transformation of such properties occur. What could be less counterintuitive than this? However, let us not miss the subtle insight enfolded in this simple truth. Any student of the history of systems of exchange will acknowledge as uncontroversial the claim that if we define a market as a space of exchange, we must understand the process and contractual terms under which the commensurability, or equivalence, between an object and its price is achieved, and on which the entirety of the exchange is predicated. After all, if money-mediated exchange is fundamentally the realization of a *symmetry* between an economic object and its image of value as money as they are transformed from one to another place in the economic space we call a market, are we not justified in wanting to know more about both the structure to such spaces, and the behavior-defining conditions such structures impose on the economic properties of the objects exchanged therein?

For example, we know that medieval-era bans of usury involved a prohibition on the growth in value of the image of the object; but wherever we see the advent of generic financial debt-transactions, we witness a loosening on this invariance requirement.[2] Likewise, any given synthetic financial transaction places its own invariance requirements on a variety of properties of the asset involved, but which are qualitatively different from and indeed much more relaxed than those of a debt or equity transaction, which is to say the kinds of exchange specific to generic finance.

And yet we also have no trouble conceding that despite qualitatively different invariance requirements marking different classes of exchange, a basic symmetry between the object and its image of value is always achieved. In fact, as we turn our thinking towards a study of the ontology of economic objects more generally, we will notice that there is always included a set of invariance requirements placed by different kinds of exchange on the properties of the objects involved therein; and that it is therefore never a matter of whether or not symmetry is actually achieved – that symmetry is achieved goes without saying;

without it no price will be agreed to, no exchange will occur. Rather, exchange *writ large* is always a matter of the amount and kind of symmetry realized in the economic space of a market, and every class of economic objects is marked by a specific set of invariance requirements placed on the behavior of its properties. Different economic objects, with different economic properties, therefore belong to a class of exchange contingent to what happens to their properties in the space (market) of their transformation (exchange).

From the first instances of *classical exchange*, to *generic finance*, to now *synthetic finance* we will see this is true. For example, classical exchange requires the congruent and immediate settlement of physical objects for their images of value as money: this is an invariance requirement on the property of tenure, which to begin with is always defined as immediate settlement – and which in turn is why it is incomprehensible to propose to consider the economic properties of maturity, interest rate, or default risk, and so on, in a classical exchange; while in generic finance this invariance requirement on tenure – defined as immediate settlement – is loosened, the properties of maturity and interest rate now differentiate themselves, and the image of the value of the object is free to grow or shrink over the time-horizon of the exchange; and once more now in synthetic finance, the invariance requirements placed on the generic financial object are loosened even more so, and as we will see, new economic properties again differentiate in the synthetic object, which are free to even more radically warp and bend, fold over and twist.

What, if any, is the historical-materialist significance of this progressive loosening of invariance requirements concomitant with the proliferation of new economic properties unknown to ostensibly prior classes of exchange, i.e., classical exchange and generic finance? And how do we register the subsequent augmentation in symmetry of the economic objects belonging to the class of exchange we know as generic finance, which historically differentiates itself at different times and places from out of classical exchange, and then again now as synthetic finance differentiates itself from out of generic finance? What does this augmented symmetry signal?

iii. The title of our opening essay indicates that we are interested in some material properties of the class of exchange of synthetic finance. A first question then is to where we look, analytically, theoretically, methodologically, as we enter the general ontological domain of finance *writ large* – when all values of objects are values as assets, and the economic properties of such assets are independent of any physicality? Is this not a question of and for materialism? As we pivot our own analysis along Tobin *et al.*'s coordinates, we will notice that the material properties of financial assets are progressively marked by an increased fungibility – and that this is especially true of synthetic financial assets; and that, moreover, the latter involve a kind of exchange that is marked by symmetry, yes, as is all exchange, but now a qualitatively different kind of symmetry than the classical symmetry realized in the exchange of either physical assets or generic financial assets. For this reason we quickly realize that an examination of the ontology of synthetic finance already requires that we move beyond Tobin *et al.*'s abstract definitions of the properties of financial assets, and that to adequately appraise the properties of many of the assets populating today's financial markets we must look elsewhere for the appropriate analytical tools.

To our knowledge there are two other thinkers who share our curiosity of the ontology of finance, and who are capable of aiding us as we enter the peculiar ontological domain of synthetic finance: Gilles Deleuze, who, in his book *Difference & Repetition* (1967) elaborates the unconventional material properties of the synthetic as a pure difference without concept; and Fischer Black, who, in his essay 'Fundamentals of Liquidity' (1970) early on emphasized the hyperfungibility marking synthetic finance, and its profound consequences for our concept of materiality. Deleuze is a French philosopher, Black an American economist; from our perspective they are philosophers of finance; we will allow each to comment on the properties we examine throughout.

iv. In order to deepen our opening attempt to investigate the ontology of synthetic finance, in Essay Two we pursue a case study on credit derivatives, which are seven notes on an object of synthetic finance par excellence. Therein we will further and more concretely illustrate for our reader the peculiar materiality exhibited by the properties of synthetic financial assets, which we will have already begun to observe in Essay One. And yet we will ultimately see that this peculiar kind of materiality does match its elegant physical simulacra with a seductive promise, or wager, which our reader may be interested to investigate further.

v. For this reason, Essay Three will propose *speculative materialism* as a method of doing heterodox political economy, and *speculative materialist communism* as a mode of economic distribution. The latter is not to be confused with a sedentary communism, which conservatively proposes a redistribution of objects in a preproduced space. Rather, we propose a radical nomadic distribution of economic space itself, founded in and by a market-based mode of exchange, but emancipated from the State-organized systemic violence of capitalism. Both of these proposals, we will show, are commensurate with our present financial technological and institutional moment. Both proposals admittingly amount to an initial sketch of statements to be expanded and detailed in forthcoming work, most immediately in our forthcoming book, titled *Infinite Leverage*.

vi. We have also attached five Appendices to the end of our three Essays in order to conceptually clarify our method further still.

If, as Spinoza maintained, the question of ethics is always a question 'of what are you capable, what can you do?' we must seek to continually pose this same question to our financial technologies and institutions as we examine their material properties. To ask and begin to address this question is the collective purpose of our three Essays and five Appendices herein.

Notes

1 James Tobin, 'Properties of Assets,' in *Money, Credit, and Capital*, McGraw Hill, 1981, p. 11.

2 For example, see Raymond De Roover, *The Medici Bank*, New York University Press, 1948, and *L'évolution de la lettre de change (XIVe-XVIIIe siècles)*, S.E.V.P.E.N, 1953.

1 Some material properties of synthetic finance

Let us consider some properties of financial assets. We will consider *moneyness*, *divisibility*, *reversibility*, *liquidity*, *maturity*, *risk*, and *cash flow*.

Moneyness

i. While money and moneyness are alike, they are not the same. Moneyness is a property of any financial asset that is not money, but is capable of being used as a medium of exchange.

Treasury bills, demand deposits, and other money market instruments are good examples of assets obtaining this property. They are in no way exhaustive of the list.

ii. In his essay, 'Properties of Assets,'[1] James Tobin does not explicitly mention moneyness (for more on this, please see 'Liquidity'), but for historical reasons this is unsurprising: prior to the mid-1970s, commercial banks were the only institutions using their balance sheets to create assets capable of being used as money. Only with recent structural transformations to the nature of interrelations between money markets and capital markets – accompanying the symbiotic proliferation of money market funds and securitization – do we witness the arrival of a new mode of financial production for the creation of wholly new kinds of assets capable of 'acting as money.'

Observation of this change is so foundational to understanding present-day finance capitalism that Allan Malz, in his big book on financial risk, now even hyperbolizes the ready availability of this property, saying: '*To the extent that an asset has the characteristics of immediacy and certainty, they resemble money and are said to be liquid.*'[2] We should not too quickly move past the understated profundity embedded in Malz's overstatement, and for this reason will later return to it when examining financial assets whose exchange lacks immediacy, i.e., whose invariance requirement on the property of tenure has been loosened beyond immediate settlement, the risk and uncertainty of the asset's value produced as a result, and its concrete consequences for liquidity (please see 'Maturity').

For now we simply note that it is always interesting to observe the coming-and-going of the moneyness of an asset when, for whatever reason, the collective will of the money market either becomes anxious over the sudden devaluation of the asset, or is unable to ascertain its value with confidence, such that the asset quickly loses its ability to act as liquid collateral (we then say that the asset is no longer capable of 'behaving like money'). Notably, for instance, we saw this at the onset of the 2007–2008 financial crisis, when ABCP (asset-backed commercial paper) and their synthetic counterparts (credit linked notes (CLNs)) were sure and acceptable collateral in the repo market – until all of a sudden they were not, as moneyness vanished from such assets, the velocity of money drastically declined, the entire balance of payments system of the money market began to short-circuit, and along with it the cessation of the circulation of debt *that is* present-day finance capitalism.[3]

iii. Marx said nothing about moneyness, nothing relevant about Treasuries, and most innovations in cash- and synthetic-securitized collateral antedate his thought. However, he did observe that money, fundamentally, is an image of value of an economic object; and much of his subsequent thinking on commodity fetishism follows from the imagistic character of money. All of *Capital*'s horrific depictions of the bizarre behavior of physical assets (e.g., of a table getting up to walk around on its hind legs; of 20 lb of cloth turning around to talk to us; and so on) follow from the metaphysical perversion of the object's transformation into an image of value, i.e., when the natural object is transformed into an economic object, and that object is exchanged for money.

In this light, it is interesting to increasingly see the property of moneyness now readily adhere to a financial asset when for whatever contingent, normative, or transitory reason it 'resembles' money 'enough' so as to behave 'as if' it *were* money; or conversely, to no longer 'resemble' money 'enough' in order to continue 'acting like it.'

What is the material significance that a class of financial assets does or does not obtain the property of moneyness? And what, if anything, does it mean, historically, that an object whose image of value *is* money now obtains an economic property allowing it to act as if it were an object for an image of the value of objects?

If money is the first financial asset, perhaps it should not surprise us when, acting as the image of value for an economic object, money now seeks out an object in its own image *capable of acting as an image for its own object*. At any rate, the progressive and regressive possibilities for the moneyness property of financial assets gives us a first glimpse into their primal but fickle fungibility. The relative amount of *fungibility* of a financial asset must be understood when considering the composition of its properties, and subsequently, when determining what is its respective class of exchange.

Divisibility

i. Divisibility is a property that denotes the availability of varieties of denominations of a financial asset, and therefore the minimum and maximum possible size for its liquidation.

The values of financial assets are denominated in money, but such assets lack many of the obvious constraints affecting other physicality: e.g., that I tear up into pieces or otherwise obliterate the document of a financial contract, for instance a Treasury bond, it neither ceases to exist nor does its value depreciate in the least.

Because money is numerical, and numbers are divisible, there are no natural or endogenous constraints on the divisibility of financial assets.

ii. We know that the wider the variety of an asset's possible denominations, the more divisible it is, and vice versa. And intuitively, we realize that access by a class of investors to a type of financial asset is partially predicated on its divisibility. However, while it is the case that a deposit, for instance, is infinitely divisible down to a penny, it is curious that most generic financial assets have traditionally come in strict, fixed denominations, and with varying sizes but a rigid invariance requirement placed on their divisibility.

For example, commercial paper is usually denominated in increments of $25,000; serial corporate bond par-values will differ in their amounts, but have traditionally only been made available in large increments; a bank loan is approved by the lender in any amount, but unless syndicated, it is indivisible and thus unavailable to most investors; a non-securitized mortgage loan is absolutely indivisible; and so on.

Tobin, too, presumes the restricted divisibility of most generic financial assets, which excludes their access to certain classes of investors (he notes, 'bonds, stocks, commodities, and durable goods...come in units of significant value relative to the wealth of many actual or potential investors, and it is either impossible or costly to sell or to buy in fractions'[4]). Consequently, he has very little to say about it as a property.

iii. We observed that availability of a type of financial asset to a class of investors is partially determined by its divisibility. And we can relatedly observe that divisibility informs the fungibility of a class of assets – since denomination is a function of numbers, since numbers as money are the original entities capable of mutual substitution (e.g., 2 $5s for a $10, etc.), and since 'a capacity for mutual substitution' is the very definition of fungibility. However, when we begin to more closely examine its property, we become increasingly aware that divisibility is often much more than a matter of simple division. An additional interesting question convoked by the property of divisibility is therefore not merely whether a particular financial asset can be divided, but *whether it will change in kind when it does*?

For example, I am entirely unimpressed if I receive a letter informing me that my round lot of Walt Disney Co. (DIS) stock has again been split, this time 2-for-1, so that now I own 200 shares at $25.00 per share, rather than 100 shares at $50.00 per share. For here there will have been the division of a generic financial asset of 1 share of stock now into 2 – yet there will have been no change in kind.

By contrast, in the *Gospel of Matthew*, Christ and his disciples have been backed against the water's edge by hungry and raucous masses, when Christ repeatedly splits two fish and five loaves, and distributes the surplus out among the crowd (and at that, after feeding them all still has a surplus of twelve full baskets!). This is the miracle of multiplication through division, an example of a nonadditive cause of added-value ex nihilo through the operation of divisibility. There are, of course, available financial corollaries to this theological example: arbitrage securitization and exchange-traded funds are two technologies whose manner of assembling debt and/or equity, respectively, both allows them to cut across generic and synthetic financial classes of exchange, as well as to augment a net asset value – through processes of division and circulation – that is higher than when in their indivisible incarnations.

Traditional finance theory simply calls this 'arbitrage,' and/or often acclaims the nonadditive material capacities of leverage, therein classing such instances with other instances of perceived like-phenomena. However, for us this betrays a glimpse of the radical material capacities of nomadic distribution.[5] For this and other reasons we will first pursue this aforementioned concept in our case study in Essay Two. And then in Essay Three, we will further elaborate the distinction between sedentary distribution (a redistribution of preproduced economic space) and nomadic distribution (a distribution of economic space itself), in order to illustrate that 'arbitrage,' as labeled here, is merely a subclass of a more general, ontologically fundamental kind of distribution that is nomadic – i.e., that nomadic distribution is nonadditive, divergent, ordinal, radical. However, presently we are simply reminded of Deleuze's observation that there are two kinds of multiplicities: numerical multiplicities, which divide without changing in kind; and qualitative multiplicities, which in the process of their division do change in kind. For this reason, too, Essay Three will also examine this ontological distinction made by Deleuze, but now as applied to financial assets and the markets they populate.

Reversibility

i. There is an operation, turnaround, or 'round-trip' cost to investing-in-and-then-out-of a financial asset. Reversibility is the property of an asset denoting such cost.

Standardized investment instruments with 'thick' and organized markets will often result in the diminution of price variability of a financial asset, and therefore exhibit little market-making risk, compared to customized (bespoke) instruments traded on 'thin' markets, with greater price variability and a higher risk of widening bid-ask spreads.

For example, Treasury bills enjoy the thickest market in world (e.g., they trade in the largest volume and on a continual 24-hour basis), and consequently maintain greater price stability; they also therefore obtain a high amount of reversibility. Contrarily, speculative tradings in the stock of a small market-cap company or in some exotic instrument often have much 'thinner' markets, whose price movements exhibit greater variability; such assets therefore obtain much less reversibility.

ii. Tobin notes that '[s]ome assets are completely irreversible. They cost something to acquire: but the holder, once he has acquired them, cannot turn them into cash in any way.'[6]

We wonder here whether, and if so how much it matters, that while this assertion today may in some instances still be true, it is also the case that it is comparatively much less true – and increasingly so?

For example, should we attempt to draw out some broader systemic significance or extract a 'deeper' historical meaning from the fact that Tobin cites as cases of 'completely irreversible' financial assets 'the rights to retirement and death benefits purchased by contributions to certain retirement programs,' when Swiss Reinsurance Co. and others like it have now commoditized such assets, imbuing them with reversibility?[7] Does it matter that in the late 1960s Tobin is able to confidently assert that 'these rights cannot be sold or assigned to anyone else, or surrendered for cash, or used as security for a loan,' when today these aforementioned restrictions on the use of such assets have been loosened, and are becoming progressively ever more loosened?

Moreover, we wish to alert our reader to yet another contemporary contradiction to an example provided by Tobin. The following example is even more instructive of our general thesis about the increasing fungibility of financial assets, but now also revelatory of a synthetic symmetry realized in an act of exchange that ontologically differs in kind from other generic financial transactions of the type with which Tobin concerns himself.

It is notable that Tobin asks his reader to compare, 'for example, a nonmarketable ten-year government savings bond with only one year left until maturity. The owner can convert it into cash at a stated value. But no one can purchase a nine-year-old savings bond.' Therefore, Tobin concludes, '[t]he measure of reversibility can be set at 0 percent in this case.' In other words, because there is no secondary market for it, the generic financial asset of a nine-year-old savings bond is, as Tobin rightly deduces, illiquid to the point of irreversibility.

But again it is interesting to observe – and perhaps the real question is whether it is *more than interesting to observe* – that contemporary innovations in financial technologies now do permit this kind of transaction, albeit not with whole or totalized economic objects, but rather with partial economic objects, shreds or fragments of objects – which is to say by replicating originally whole objects whose economic properties have been divided and repeated, therein changing such objects and their properties in kind. What do we mean? In this case, for example, the synthetic financial asset of a credit default swap (CDS) allows for the equivalent sale or purchase of the properties of risk and cash flow of a nine-year-old savings bond (for more on credit derivatives please see Essay Two herein). One may choose to call it a 'mere simulation' or 'replication' of such sale or purchase; but its transaction risk, yield, cash flow, maturity, and other economic properties may be tailored to reproduce or differ from those of the nine-year-old savings bond, such that there is or is not an important material distinction between the two.

This is to say that we are justified to assert that Tobin is still correct that a generic financial asset, such as a nine-year-old savings bond, is indeed lacking the property of reversibility – for this particular invariance requirement still governs the symmetry of this group of objects, and belonging to its class of exchange, which is generic finance. But we are also justified to assert that, contrary to Tobin, today there are increasingly less obstacles to investing in the equivalent of purchasing a nine-year-old bond, provided we understand what precisely has occurred in such a synthetic transaction, and what is its resulting material effects.

iii. There are three preliminary points to make here, to which we will return in our case study in Essay Two, wherein we begin to more deliberately reflect on the material consequences of the fact that, given the ostensibly unbounded capacities of synthetic financial engineering, there is no endogenous constraint on the attainment of the property of reversibility.

First, a historical observation. If today's financial assets are not merely increasingly divisible, as we observed above, but now increasingly reversible as well, we should grasp the significance of both of these subplots against the more general backdrop of the progressive fungibility of financial assets. This quantitative increase in fungibility is a structural change to the ontology of financial assets that in our view demands further examination, insofar as it accompanies the progressive differentiation of finance as a system as a whole.[8] The science of morphogenesis tells us that in the course of the development of any dynamical system, the price paid for a structure of order is a loss of symmetry, and subsequent quantitative diminution in fungibility. How, then, is it that the progressive differentiation of our financial system entails the acquisition of both a higher degree of symmetry and more fungibility?

Second, an ontological observation. While the synthetic equivalent of purchasing or selling a nine-year-old bond by way of its replication through a credit default swap is, as we have observed, in many ways a repetition of the same, it is important to note that there are nonetheless *some* material differences between the generic financial version in the nine-year-old bond and its synthetic incarnation of a CDS. There is a difference produced by its repetition.

We have already alluded to this difference in repetition above, and will have opportunity to more carefully unpack this point in our case study in Essay Two, as well as to illustrate the meaning of its profound ontology in Essay Three. But even immediately here, our reader will acknowledge that while to begin with the CDS is ostensibly a synthetic copy of the generic model, a 'mere' derivative of the so-called 'referent' or 'underlying' generic financial asset, it does have the added virtue of obtaining the property of reversibility, and therefore both enjoys a looser set of invariance requirements than those governing the equivalent exchange of its generic financial counterpart, but also therefore has different –and meaningfully different – economic properties than the generic asset it proposes to 'merely' repeat.

To be sure, a symmetry is actualized in both the purchase/sale of a generic bond and the purchase/sale of a CDS on that bond; and the latter, as we observed, can be written to either (synthetically) replicate or modify the cash flow, notional value, kind of risk exposure, maturity, etc. of the former. But what is the material difference between these two classes of assets?

From one point of view, we may be tempted to say that both transactions accomplish the same thing – albeit the bond transaction is the generic 'model,' and the CDS is the synthetic (and so-called) 'copy' of the model. However, because the synthetic transaction maintains a more relaxed set of invariance requirements on its reversibility (as well as other properties, as we will see in our case study in Essay Two), and is consequently more fungible even as it actualizes a *synthetic kind of symmetry that is a symmetry nonetheless*, we are much closer to the truth when we say that *there is a qualitative difference in kind* marking this synthetic repetition of the supposedly 'more original' generic financial transaction of the bond. In this respect, in a very concrete sense, the peculiar materiality of the synthetic financial transaction has upended the grounds on which any clear distinction between a copy and its model would stand.

Deleuze has observed that what marks the peculiar materiality of the property of the synthetic is its ontological status as image without likeness.[9] It is precisely this qualitative difference between the material properties of generic financial assets and synthetic financial assets that we must examine in more depth. What is the meaning of a synthetic symmetry that now reveals a glimpse of itself from within and out of generic finance as a class of exchange, but which also increasingly transcends the invariance requirements of the latter, thereby imbuing the newly differentiated and prior economic properties of financial assets with both a quantitative increase in fungibility and a qualitatively more original symmetry than their generic ontological counterpart and historical predecessor?

What more, then, if anything, is instructive for us about the property of reversibility?

Third, let us stop to draw a general and preliminary conclusion for our nascent methodology, whose outline we will continue to sketch throughout Essays One, Two, and Three, and in the Appendices.

We will see that it is much more remarkable than at first glance that reversibility, while obviously quite capable of adhering to a financial asset *as a property*, is most certainly not an inherent property of any asset, per se, but rather is a property whose existence as a property is always determined by exogenous and floating conditions (e.g., thickness vs. thinness of the market; price volatility; risk of widening bid-ask-spreads; time costs, commission costs, delivery costs, etc. of market making; a lack or availability of technology for synthetic replication; and so on), which are largely independent of, though certainly not unrelated to it.

In fact, the heuristics of our opening exercise of ontologically sifting through some properties of financial assets more generally leads us to observe something that is perhaps already obvious to our reader – if also, we expect, its extended consequences have hitherto often been underappreciated: namely, there is no property of a financial asset that is inherent to it or 'in-itself,' since the properties of financial assets are only ever acquired or lost relative to their transformation in the space of exchange we call a market.

Pedagogical purposes endemically require that in Essay Two we examine the synthetic asset *as an object*. And yet this is already problematic. As our cursory study of the ontological differences between the nine-year-old savings bond and its synthetic replication already shows, we are proceeding backwards if we begin with an analysis of the asset as a static object, and from there attempt to move forward with an examination of its properties – as if the actuality of the asset, its physicality, and other immaterial properties held any economic importance whatsoever.

In point of fact this manner of doing political economy has too often contaminated its methodology, causing its discipline to continually work with an absurdly and ironically labeled 'materialist analysis,' when all along its analysis was never materialist enough. Our position is that this is a consequence of a bad ontology, which has and will continue to produce zero insight into our contemporary economic state of affairs, will leave us ignorant of how to use the economic objects already lying around us, and will ultimately leave it impotent to discover what more our financial instruments are actually capable of doing, but which they presently in fact are not.

Rather, because it is the case that paradoxically the asset *is* its properties while yet these properties pledge no allegiance to their asset; because such properties must adhere to an asset in order to actualize themselves, and yet are never absolutely contained, controlled, or commanded by the asset; and because such properties are always floating, fleeting, and contingent to their asset, a true materialist analysis of the properties of financial assets requires that we first wholesale revise our understanding *of what precisely 'materialism' is*? This can only be done by first dispensing with the notion that assets have essences – even if this is only ever implicitly assumed, it is assumed nonetheless. And this can only be done by thinking of the assets and the markets they populate as multiplicities.

Only in proceeding in this way can political economy ever hope to (re)gain its scientific footing, and shed its immaterialist and analytically emaciated asset-fetishism (for more on asset-fetishism and revising our definition of materialism, please see 'Liquidity,' 'Risk,' and especially 'Cash Flow'). For this reason, by the end of Essay Three we will have realized why, in regarding financial assets, we are always already regarding multiplicities.

Liquidity

i. It is not easy to overstate our difficulty arriving at a universal definition of liquidity. Already our trouble begins when we attempt to identify the entity to which its property adheres.

For example, our commonplace expectations about the basic character of liquidity – that even if floating, contingent, or otherwise interpellated by ostensibly exogenous conditions, liquidity is nonetheless always only a property of an asset – is a view increasingly compromised by colloquial references made to a '*market's* liquidity,' or when we periodically hear of some market participant losing *his* or *her* or *its* 'funding liquidity.'

Jean Laplanche often invoked the unfinished project of the Copernican revolution; and it seems here too the spirit of such a project must proceed.[10] But even if we are willing to grant that economic properties do not so much eternally 'belong' to assets as that they constitute their plastic and decentered essence, how do we reconcile the notion of the liquidity of an asset with now the liquidity of a market, or even the liquidity of funding? Is liquidity now not exclusively, or even at all, a property of assets? And if it is not a property of assets, *where then is it when liquidity is what it is*? Of course that liquidity 'is' anything at all, which is to say the very notion that it 'is' a 'thing,' may already betray a poorly formulated problem.

It seems clear that we can no longer regard liquidity as an extensive property, or for that matter a sedentary good, i.e., a kind of property 'in' an asset –as if liquidity-flow is like a car whose driver parks it in a parking lot, but can then leave and reenter the parking lot at different speeds, based on the number and type of obstacles in its route to and from the entrance/exit. Today, we know and say that liquidity is excitable and contingent, but perhaps it is even more fleeting and ephemeral than this.

Malz's discussion of liquidity reflects this subtle but important aforementioned shift towards now our multiple usages of its concept, and which betrays its increasing ambiguity: he notes that liquidity can appear as a property of assets ('transaction liquidity': '[a]n asset is said to be liquid if it is "near" or a good substitute for cash'); but that its specter can also appear in the markets they populate ('market liquidity': '[a] market is said to be liquid if market participants can unwind positions quickly, without excessive transactions costs and without excessive price deterioration'); and it can even materialize as a property ostensibly attaching itself to a borrower ('funding liquidity': '[which is] more closely related to [a borrower's] creditworthiness … [or] ability to finance assets continuously at an acceptable borrowing rate').

How then should we understand the property of liquidity? Can we provide a universal definition capable of cutting across these three instances of its usage, i.e., when it adheres to an asset, market, or borrower? We believe we can, and that liquidity is correctly defined *as the nominal relationship between maturity and value*. Of course the very meaning of this statement requires some elaboration.

ii. Our aforementioned definition leaps from out of the body of Tobin's understanding of liquidity, though we terminologically rework it in order to release its soul.

Fabozzi *et al.* believe themselves to be following Tobin on liquidity; and as we have, they note the trouble involving attempts at its definition ('[liquidity] is an important and widely used notion, although there is at present no uniformly accepted definition'). They recommend as 'useful' the definition 'proposed by Professor James Tobin, *in terms of how much sellers stand to lose if they wish to sell immediately against engaging in a costly and time-consuming search.*'[11]

This is a poor paraphrase of Tobin and one that we cannot accept; not so much because it is inelegant as that it obfuscates what is instructive about his actual definition. To be clear, Tobin does not define liquidity '*in terms of how much sellers stand to lose if they wish to sell immediately against engaging in a costly and time-consuming search.*' He initially even hesitates to define it – and not, we are led to believe, on behalf of a prudent deference to his reader's financial literacy, but more so as an exercise of ruminating in an open and preliminary discussion of that thing called 'liquidity,' about which he is puzzled, but for which he seeks to find an adequate definition.

Tobin begins his meditation on liquidity by pointing out that the only financial asset with 'perfect liquidity' is cash-money, which he identifies as 'currency and other assets generally acceptable as means of payment.'[12] 'Indeed,' he adds, 'realization of the value of an asset means realization in cash.'[13]

By this we naturally understand Tobin to be saying that the value of an asset is realized when in its liquidated form, and its liquidated form is cash-money. The assertion appears relatively uncontroversial. However, we should observe that while empirically true, this assertion also betrays both a tautology and a paradox involving the property of liquidity: for on the one hand, the value of an asset is, of course, only ever represented and representable to us insofar as it takes the form of money, i.e., in its liquidated form, and its quantity of money is always expressed by its price; but on the other hand, liquidity is not simply or only money, since if it were, these two separate concepts would denote the same object, which they quite obviously do not.

Even superficially, that we often speak of liquidity as if it were potentially an economic property of any financial asset except money, yet whose latter essence we understand as liquidity, already conveys this paradox. But it seems there is even more to it than this.

The International Accounting Standards (IAS) implicitly acknowledges this subtle but fuzzy ontological distinction between cash-money and liquidity when it defines 'cash' vs. 'cash equivalents.' IAS defines 'cash-money': 'cash comprises cash on hand and demand deposits' (notice now the tautological nature of the definition, i.e., cash-money is cash-money, as well as deposits, which consist of cash-money). But there are also 'cash equivalents,' as in assets with *moneyness*, which are defined as: 'short term, highly liquid investments that are readily converted to known amounts of cash and which are subject to an insignificant risk in changes in value' (notice again the tautology, here: the cash equivalent asset's ability for immediate liquidation causes both its resemblance to, but also necessary distinction from money, i.e., cash equivalents are almost cash-money, can quickly become cash-money, but cannot ever actually *be* cash-money, or else they would no longer be cash equivalents, but now would be actual cash-money).[14] IAS definitions thus render 'cash' as a perfectly liquid asset in the form of money, and 'cash equivalents' as highly but not perfectly liquid assets, whose potential to achieve perfect liquidity *as money* remains latent but always and necessarily unrealized (since again, if an asset finally achieved this potential it would now literally no longer be itself, insofar as it would now be money).

However, that Tobin and the IAS both founder here on what we have labeled both tautology and paradox – whereby liquidity *qua* money is merely the necessary form taken by a liquidated asset, and yet liquidity is both other-than-but-somehow-also-nothing-more-than a property of an asset when the asset is in its non-liquidated (i.e., non-moneyed) form – is less a testament to analytical confusion on their part than it is the dark nature of our beast; our beast here being liquidity, and its beastliness residing in its metaphysically anomalous, virtual bilocation in money and asset alike, yet in full actuality simultaneously extensively disembodied of either.

For again, if liquidity *is* money that is virtual and latent in an asset, it can only *be*, as such, when that asset is not actually in its moneyed form. For when liquidity 'becomes' money, the asset's liquidity is itself liquidated, it vanishes in the process. Liquidity in actuality thus necessarily always falls just short of being money; and an asset can never be completely perfect in its liquidity or else it would now be money. In this respect, liquidity appears to be what thermodynamics, Deleuze, and dynamical systems theory label an 'intensive property.' Indeed, it is the intensive corollary to the extensive property of price denoted in money, insofar as it covers over or cancels itself out in the process of actualizing its liquidation in and as money; it is also not so much indivisible as that which divides, but when dividing always changes in kind.

iii. Tobin – who at this point has still not defined liquidity – obviously has no intention to confront its paradox, tautology, or peculiar metaphysics. He provides his readers with a graph in order that we might better visualize the representational dynamics of liquidity (for pedagogical purposes we have reproduced but slightly tweaked and added on to this graph below) (Figure 1.1).

We will shortly consider Tobin's definition of liquidity, which he only backs his way into near the end of his discussion, and whose curious materiality we both wish to probe and then analyze in relation to the properties of maturity, risk, and cash flow below.

Before he actually defines liquidity, though, Tobin uses the graph in Figure 1.1 to *describe* it as a property whose presence in assets progressively and regressively accumulates in quantity – first as *cash-money* (the instantiation of 'perfect liquidity'), then presumably to assets with *moneyness* (what IAS calls 'cash equivalents'), and from there a number of factors determine the relative 'perfection' and 'imperfection' of the liquidity of any given financial asset.

Brief consideration of this graph is instructive for our understanding of the intensive property of liquidity. Tobin:

> At a given moment of time an asset has a certain full value. But the percentage of this value that can actually be realized will generally depend on how long ago the decision to sell the asset was realized. This relationship between the realized price of the asset and the length of time the decision to sell preceded the actual sale can be shown graphically.[15]

We wish to alert our reader that later, when considering the property of cash flow, we will return to the belief professed by Tobin in this aforementioned quote in order to observe *that* and *why* Fischer Black vehemently disparages this very notion as naïve, immaterialist, and symptomatic of what we have labeled 'asset-fetishism': given that it is not the asset, per se, but rather its cash flow that has value; and acknowledging the progressive trend towards a complete absence of endogenous limitations to the absolute fungibility of synthetic financial assets, Black observes that there is no necessary relation between an asset's realized value *as* price and its liquidity.

However, relatedly and preliminarily, we must first complete our consideration of Tobin's discussion – wherein liquidity indubitably *does* inform the realization of value as the price of an asset.

Let us observe that since the obvious purpose of this graph is to depict the property of liquidity, the reader quickly realizes that in the quote we reproduced above, Tobin has surreptitiously already begun to define liquidity (namely, as 'th[e] relationship between the realized price of the asset and the length of time the decision to sell preceded the actual sale'), without yet announcing that this is what he is doing.

We are also immediately struck here by the sudden appearance of heavy intonations of the ontologically weighty concept of time: e.g., 'at a given moment,' 'how long ago,' and 'length of time,' are all, according to Tobin, intimately related to the asset's value. More specifically, we cannot overlook that as Tobin begins to covertly edge his way towards providing a formal definition of liquidity, he suddenly

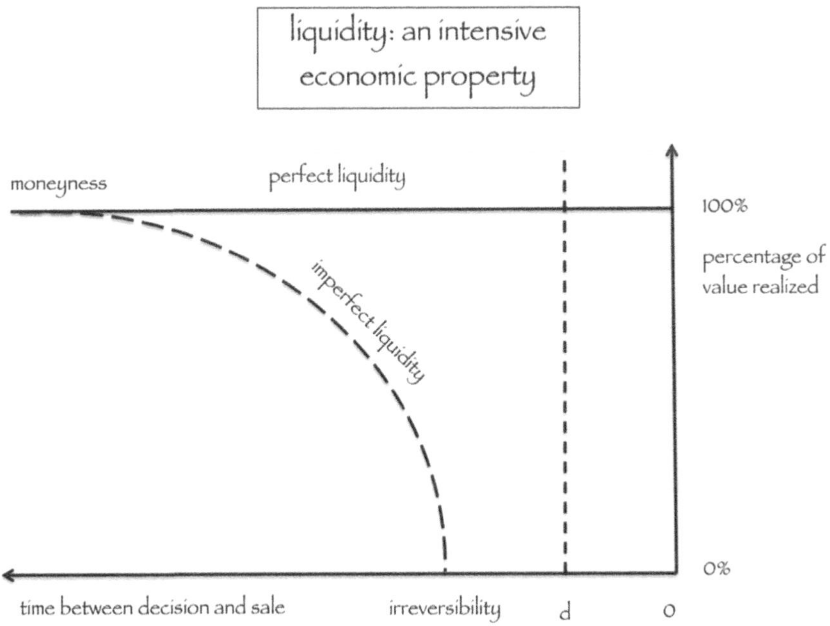

Figure 1.1 Liquidity: an intensive economic property.

finds himself needing to invoke the property of maturity as now an additional property whose force affects the other properties of a financial asset, as the asset is transformed in-and-over the course of the space-time of the exchange.

Tobin proceeds to explain the elements of his graph.

At one end of the graph we see a line marking perfect liquidity:

> a perfectly liquid asset is represented by a horizontal line at 100 percent, meaning that no matter how recently the decision to sell the asset was reached, the full value of the asset can be realized.[16]

Let us say that a symmetry has been realized between an asset and its image of value as money; and the subsequent economic transformation of an exchange has occurred. 'Perfect liquidity' here denotes *that the time-horizon on the maturity of the exchange does not cause any depreciation in the image of the value of the asset* when it is sold and thereby transformed into its image of value as money.

What, then, of imperfect liquidity?

Cutting its way through the middle of Tobin's graph we see the curve of imperfect liquidity:

> the curve marked 'imperfect liquidity' depicts a different kind of asset. Its full value can be realized only if sufficient time is allowed to find a buyer. With shorter notice, up to a limit, the asset can be sold, but less will be realized the later the decision was reached.[17]

Here, again, let us say that a symmetry has been realized, and the subsequent economic transformation of an exchange has occurred. But now we see that, in this case, the transaction involves the exchange of an 'imperfectly liquid' asset –and the asset is imperfectly liquid precisely because *it does experience some depreciation to its image of its value as money over the time-horizon of the maturity of the exchange.*

In this sense, it is clear that liquidity is a desirable property for an asset to obtain: it determines, or at least largely informs, the relative resilience of the asset to the risk embedded in the maturity of exchange – and more specifically the risk that the image of value of the object will depreciate over the time-period between the decision to sell the asset, and the commencement and termination of the actual sale itself. In this respect as well, we see once more that liquidity is a property that defines the relation between risk and realized value as price, and yet cancels itself out in the process of actualizing the quality of their relationship.

iv. To concretely illustrate his coherent but otherwise somewhat abstract description, Tobin provides as an example 'the imperfect liquidity of a house, in contrast to the perfect liquidity of a listed security,' noting that the amount of liquidity adhering to each asset 'is a consequence of several factors.'[18]

Such factors will now be familiar to our reader, for they are roughly the same factors we earlier observed as the exogenous conditions interpellating reversibility – e.g., thinness of markets (Tobin calls it 'infrequency of trading' and 'scarcity of buyers'), disorganized and/or slow communication, risk of widening bid-ask spreads, and so on. However, by far the most important factor for Tobin in determining the relative liquidity of any given asset is 'the differentiation of particular assets from each other.' And fortuitously, nowhere is this clearer than in Tobin's comparative example of a house and a share of stock – for here we have an imperfectly liquid, indivisible, utterly differentiated, and singular asset (house) standing in stark contrast to a highly liquid, highly divisible, non-differentiated, and standardized asset (stock share):

> Whereas one share of IBM stock is exactly like every other share, no one house is exactly like any other. Each particular house is only occasionally on the market; some shares of IBM are always for sale. While the price of IBM stock is being established hour by hour in actual exchanges, the market price of a particular house is not continuously available. Its value must be learned from experience with potential buyers once the house has been put up for sale. Nor will the potential buyers appear at once. The spread of information is imperfect and slow.[19]

Our case study in Essay Two involves a more in-depth discussion of securitization, or structured finance, which is a technology for commoditizing, dividing, de-differentiating, re-differentiating, and therefore standardizing as securities any financial asset – which in this case is a house – and we will therein have occasion to reflect on the material impact of the regressive differentiation of mortgage-debt as now a group of economic objects known as asset-backed-securities, and a class of exchange unto itself.

For now, however, we will simply note that the 'one-share-like-every-other' quality of IBM stock versus the 'every-one-unlike-any-other' quality of a house is both a crucial point for Tobin – since it illustrates the profound ontological effect of the *becoming-liquid* of a financial asset in the course of its exchange[20] – and is a crucial point for us as well, since it returns us once more to our original concern with the moneyness property of assets, wherein different financial assets with their dissimilar economic properties suddenly become absolutely non-differentiated insofar as they are considered 'enough like' money to 'act as money.'

Again, how are we to understand the meaning of this movement of the economic property of liquidity towards moneyness, i.e., as if the economic properties of a given asset become increasingly undifferentiated, until finally that asset 'is' actualized as money? And what, if any, are its consequences for our existing analysis of the progressive fungibility of financial assets?

Tobin's simple contrast of the differentiated house and the undifferentiated generic share of stock reveals that if our colloquial concept of liquidity denotes the potential melting-down, as in the liquidation, or rather the becoming-liquid of an asset's properties now into the image of its value in money, it is only insofar as all other material differences between qualitatively distinct assets become utterly undifferentiated in the very act of exchange. In fact, only because this is the case is it even comprehensible for Tobin to speak of financial assets as ascending and descending on a graduated scale of liquidity: first as money, then to moneyness, then to the highly liquid, then to the moderately liquid, then to the moderately illiquid, then to the highly illiquid, and finally to irreversibility.[21]

Now, if liquidity truly is a property that augments and dissipates on a graduated scale from nondifferentiation to differentiation, this may cause us to believe that 'the amount' of liquidity 'in' an asset acts as a kind of measurement, or proxy for the market's relative indifference to the material differences in properties between various financial assets – again, such as, in this instance, the various material differences between a house and a share of stock, or even the ultimate undifferentiated asset of money itself. And in a very superficial respect, it may. However, we should take note here that we often say, but merely as a manner of speaking, that an 'asset' or 'market' *is* liquid, or that a borrower *has* 'funding liquidity' – since we well know what this truly signifies: in truth, it is in every case *the transaction, or the exchange (of the asset for its image of value) itself which has liquidity*, not the asset, market, or to-be-(re)funded-individual, per se: *it is the act or operation of the exchange which has liquidity.*

And so this once again leads us to conclude that while we commonly speak of economic properties – in this case the property of liquidity – attaching or adhering *to* an asset, in truth such property is a property of the process of the exchange, not of the object, or of the asset, per se. For if by 'exchange' we understand the transformation of the asset into its image of value in a space we call a market, we will immediately believe that an exchange always involves the exchange of a kind of asset. But if the asset is only a kind of asset, and thus is only an asset as such insofar as it belongs to a class of exchange; and if any given class of exchange determines the invariance requirements on the economic properties of the asset; upon some critical reflection we must now realize that we are unjustified to speak objectively of kinds of assets, as having essences or final natures – since any asset is only an asset insofar as it is included in a class of exchange. The asset may retroactively always appear to contain its extensive economic properties, but this is merely a phenomenal byproduct of the exchange. In reality the asset just 'happens to be there' when the properties are transformed into their image, but in no way is it material to or informative of the exchange itself.

v. Tobin, of course, as we mentioned above, has neither the concern nor penchant to think through the ontological significance of his analysis of liquidity. It is interesting that his definition of it stumbles upon it nonetheless.

We see that Tobin inadvertently ends up backing his way into a definition of liquidity – not as a property that aptly describes an object or good, or identifies a set of fundamental subproperties in some kind of functional relationship, and which actualizes itself into the formal property of 'liquidity'; *but rather as a property which itself can only be described by a functional relationship.*

Finally at the end of his discussion Tobin defines liquidity:

> *The liquidity of an asset is a property described by a functional relationship between delay time and percentage realization.*[22]

He then adds that, importantly, the nature of this relationship is neither cardinal nor ordinal, but rather is nominal (i.e., it is 'not [described] by a single number, there may be no simple ordering of assets according to liquidity').[23]

We have said that our own definition of liquidity is *the nominal relationship between maturity and value*. And we have said that our definition leaps from out of the body of Tobin's definition, but that we first needed to terminologically liberate its soul.

For instance, our reader will notice that we have substituted 'delay-time' and 'percentage [of value] realization,' with simply 'maturity' and 'value.' In one light this is immaterial, and a matter of streamlining our definitional consistency. However, it is also important for our reader to know that, first, we understand that delay-time is a subproperty of maturity (please see 'Maturity'), and that maturity is in turn a subproperty of tenure – and so a more thorough understanding of our definition of liquidity in turn requires some elaboration of the property of maturity. Second, because we are neither openly nor covertly Platonic about value, we believe that any realization of the price of an asset is its current and nominal value, which *is* its cardinal, putative, actual value (please see 'Risk'); and that insofar as the actual value of an asset is always subject to change, to change contingently, and at any rate the cardinal value 'in' an asset is in actuality only ever the value of its collective economic properties – which, in turn, as we know, are always fleeting and in flux, and never committed once and for all to their asset – this means that cardinal value is actual value, and actual value is at once stochastic, indeterminate, and ultimately as real as a ghost.

It is perhaps a bitter pill to swallow that there is no objectively definable meaning to cardinal value, that this kind of value is not and cannot be congealed in an asset, because in fact there is no economic property 'in' any asset. The economic concept of value qua cardinal value can neither be a product of labor, nor utility, etc., which in turn could be said to accumulate and reside 'in' an object, because in fact this kind of value is a putative property, a historical concept produced by habitus, culture, and various codes of conduct that are better left to ethnographic case studies by anthropologists. To believe that cardinal value persists or in some way accumulates 'in' an asset is to both fetishize the asset and maintain an ontologically naïve understanding of materiality.

Our political economy, by contrast and to begin with, concerns itself with cash flow and its relation to the distribution of risk. We cannot, however, comprehensively discuss risk without understanding its relation to maturity, and the latter's relation to tenure.

However, we will also see that a rather unexpected yet compelling notion results from declaiming cardinal value, of dispensing with any concerted ontological examination of it, of declaring it not so much analytically false as inessential, ordinary, unimportant, and thus commencing in the fashion that we do. For we will see that by proceeding in this manner, and merely attending to our business of the study of ontology of synthetic finance, a new concept of value now begins to supervene on our analysis, if only at first as a glimmer, backhandedly, and almost inadvertently or by chance. Especially at the end of Essay Two, and then again in Essay Three, we will begin to detect a glimmer of a concept of ordinal value.

Maturity

i. Today, the property of maturity, sometimes called 'term to maturity,' is often defined as the time-horizon from the date of commencement of the exchange until its scheduled termination – whether signaled by a final (re)payment, or satisfaction of some condition of a contract whereby one or more parties to a transaction is entitled to demand liquidation.

This is a fine enough definition of maturity, though there is quite a bit more to it than this. Maturity, in truth, is a thoroughly undertheorized, poorly understood property. For example, we may wish to assert that an economy founded on classical exchange, and therefore solely exchanging physical objects, has no concept of maturity. But it is more accurate to say that in classical forms of exchange, maturity is strictly confined, or even repressed by an invariance requirement on the economic property of tenure, wherein the time-horizon of the tenure of any exchange is always restricted to immediate settlement.

Our reader may wish to know more about maturity, and for this reason we must zoom-out the aperture of our ontological lens of analysis even further still.

ii. It is not superfluous to note that a barter economy would have no actual concept of liquidity, and without liquidity there can be no concept of tenure.

Exchangeability, tradability, desirability, salability, and so on could very-well adhere to any given object as a property of that object in a non-money-mediated system of exchange – but not liquidity, whose property comes about only when, and indeed as a result of, the exchange of objects whose symmetry is achieved and expressed through the medium of money as their image of value.

Only when money-mediated forms of exchange arise does it become comprehensible to discuss the need to liquidate an economic object in its moneyed form. Conversely, only in a money-mediated system of exchange does liquidity become a hazard of trade *in time*. That is to say, only when money supplants the direct, unmediated, and necessarily immediate exchange of objects with now images of their value in price, denominated in money, whatever the form, does a discontinuous time-period and then the potential for an infinite number of extended time-horizons to an exchange even become possible; and only when exchange becomes discontinuous and temporally extended does the *risk* arise that the image of value of the object I now possess will shrink (or for the counterparty, that it will grow) over the course of time. This risk gives birth to differentiation of a new economic property that acquires a more refined temporal-dimension, rather than as had previously and exclusively been the case, a purely spatial one.

This is an elaborate way of observing that only when liquidity both allows for and creates these conditions does the concept and property of tenure materialize. And only then can the property of maturity differentiate itself from tenure, and become that version of the property we commonly understand it to be today.

iii. Heichelheim is our authority here. In his sometimes bizarre but magnificent *An Ancient Economic History*, he relays some practical problems involving early instances of non-money-mediated exchange in the Paleolithic era – which in turn led to the first documented uses of money as a medium of exchange, and along with it the birth of the property of liquidity.

Heichelheim notes that 'pure barter' often entailed long and painstaking attempts to achieve symmetry between quantitatively different amounts of qualitatively dissimilar objects, until finally both parties to the exchange were able to find goods they found useful and satisfactory:

> Consequently, society soon began, perhaps as early as the Paleolithic stage, to give preference to certain wares, which were desirable to all from religious or economic reasons. These are the beginnings of money.[24]

Heichelheim moves on to observe the varieties of respective materials used as money (i.e., 'which varies according to tribe and locality, and takes the form of plates of ostrich shells, shellfish, lumps of salt, bracelets or chains of conventional designs and material, pearls of all kinds, stones of every form, boar's tusks, elephant's tusks, or dog's teeth'),[25] and the varieties of goods bought and sold therein (whether with 'tools money,' 'clothes money,' certain 'decorative axes,' and so on).[26]

It is difficult to overstate the radical ontological significance of the invention of liquidity that accompanies the progressive differentiation of money – and more specifically, its godlike capacity to actualize symmetry between different quantities of qualitatively dissimilar objects: of streamlining exchange, of opening up its time-portal of possibilities to different maturities, and all by offering itself as a stand-in substitute for economic objects with their images of value.

However, it is equally important to observe that at this early stage in the history of *homo economicus* Paleolithic exchange still only consisted of that simple, pedestrian, and blue-collar kind of exchange we label 'classical exchange'; and that this class of exchange maintains very strict invariance requirements on the transformation of the economic properties of the objects exchanged. For example, Heichelheim takes pains to observe that money used in Paleolithic exchange was 'only used for certain purposes [insofar as] *it could not be invested with interest*, and [therefore] had only a limited economic value.'[27] And elsewhere he again emphasizes: 'All forms of money which have been mentioned so far *differ from the forms of money which we use today, because they could not be lent out for interest*.'[28]

Indeed, we know that humanity would have to await the later arrival of a new class of exchange capable of loosening this invariance requirement on the image of value of the object; and at that, which accomplished this remarkable metaphysical feat by allowing for an extension of the time-horizon of tenure to extend out into time beyond the immediate present, by loosening its previous requirement of immediate settlement – which, namely, signals the birth of generic finance, and with it the differentiation of the property of maturity.

The *general* reason why this is the case is that Paleolithic exchange was always only classical exchange – and classical exchange both stipulates the absolute fixity of the image of value of the object, and generally maintains a rigid set of invariance requirements on all of the economic properties therein (except the object's orientation: the object, of course, is allowed to reposition itself as it changes parties in the course of its exchange; this is what allows for the process of classical exchange to take flight to begin with, i.e., as a transformation of an object that is neither regarded as theft, nor gift, nor appropriation). This means that classical exchange does not allow for transactions involving debt and/or equity, not to mention credit derivatives or other synthetic assets, precisely because it maintains strict invariance requirements on the symmetry transformation we call exchange. The *specific* reason why this is the case is that chief among these invariance requirements on the economic properties is the property of tenure. And again, in Paleolithic exchange, which to begin with was only classical exchange, tenure is always restricted to and defined as immediate settlement. And while tenure cannot change, so too no property of maturity can differentiate itself from out of tenure.

iv. It is interesting to see how far removed this aforementioned invariance requirement on tenure is, when defined as immediate settlement, from our current expectation on an asset's maturity.

Fabozzi *et al.*, who are characteristically pithy, simply observe that '[maturity] can range from one day to a few decades.'[29] Tobin, no less in passing, only notes that 'no other asset [other than money] is perfectly liquid, *for there is always some delay in turning it into cash*, if only hours or minutes or seconds.'[30]

Malz at least alludes, as his historical point of departure, to the fact that liquidity infuses the possibility of discontinuity into the activity of exchange; yet he is obviously neither particularly interested to investigate its intimate relation to liquidity, nor does he seek to extract the consequences of tenure for the property of risk. For example, he observes:

> Most assets other than money do not completely share [its] characteristic of immediacy and certainty. They cannot be exchanged directly for other goods and assets, *because we don't live in a barter economy*; only money can do that. Nonmoney assets must be sold or liquidated before they can be exchanged for other goods or assets. This takes at least some time, and the proceeds from the sale are uncertain to at least some extent.[31]

There is much more to say about the property of tenure, and its relation to maturity. However, we leave these issues currently unaddressed, and will therefore only note in closing that there are a number of subproperties to the property of maturity which are typically not incorporated into the standard definition with which we commenced, but whose ontological significance our reader may wish to think through on her own. For instance, we did not discuss at length the subproperty of *time-horizon* (the duration of the exchange) in particular, since the relaxation of this invariance requirement on maturity best captures the essential shift from the immediate exchange of physical objects marking classical exchange to now debt-transactions and other generic financial forms of exchange.

Tobin, to his credit, for instance, also mentions *delay-time* (the time-period between the decision to sell and the actual sale itself), which is another subproperty of maturity.[32] We could certainly elaborate others.

Our reader by now, however, will grasp our point: we have observed that liquidity in some sense truly *is* the original source of fungibility, its essence and creator. But the price paid for such fungibility – and by virtue of the possibilities for discontinuity that liquidity introduces into the time-horizon of the exchange – is a new kind of risk now embedded in maturity: the risk that the image of the object I hold in my hand, at my bank, in my portfolio, or on my balance sheet, will depreciate in time. This risk is a risk that is primal to generic finance.

Risk

i. Uncertainty of the value of assets that mature in the future is widely understood to be a property of all financial assets. It is also a general definition of financial risk.

The standard model of risk measurement originally developed by modern finance theory studies how to quantify *market risk* in particular. Its shortcomings have been articulated, often from within modern finance theory itself, and usually derive from the critique that its concept of risk is simply not robust enough to capture the totality of risks contingently attaching themselves to an asset. For this reason, and because its models of price behavior achieve normally distributed returns, but profound evidence from episodes of financial crises (among other less notable events) have established that returns are often not normally distributed, alternative approaches (e.g., jump-diffusion models, extreme value theory, behavioralist models, and so on) continue to supplement or even supplant the standard model today.

However, despite these apparent differences in method, a commonality threading through the entirety of modern finance theory is its epistemological approach to risk. By contrast, we are unapologetically interested in its ontology.

ii. It is the case that when attempting to move our thinking beyond mere epistemology and on to the business of an ontology of finance we are less interested in names of persons, established discourse, and ideologies than we are in mobile structures, decentered objects, processes, and their n-dimensional interrelations. However, the contribution by Harry Markowitz is instructive for our preexisting line of thought, and deserves a brief comment herein.

It is well known that Markowitz's 1952 paper inaugurated modern finance theory by providing the original epistemological insight that the property of risk – and not simply expected return, cash flow, yield, and the other ostensible elements of price performance – was relevant to the composition of an optimally efficient portfolio. Markowitz pointed out that the amount of risk infusing a portfolio depends on the dynamic covariance *among* or *between* its total assets, rather than the average risk 'of' or 'in' its separate assets; and only because of this observation are we today capable of understanding that an efficiently diversified portfolio is one which has achieved an optimal amount of return for a given degree of risk, or a minimum degree of risk for a desired optimal return.

It truly is a brilliant little move. Once Markowitz's concept of efficiency is understood, unsystematic risk – the promise goes – can be isolated from systematic market risk, and the latter is then definable as that leftover kind of risk that cannot be diversified-away; we have therefore achieved a profound epistemological insight, which then gives birth to the whole conceptual apparatus of modern finance theory that follows, e.g., CAPM's beta, Wiener processes, and affiliated technical concepts, not to mention Black and Scholes's bold promise of our ability to construct a zero-beta portfolio – which, *if universally achieved*, in theory, if not in practice as well, would eliminate all risk, in turn removing the pricing mechanism for valuation of financial assets, and thus put into question the very basic character of finance, as such. If continuous arbitrage is both impossible *and* the condition of possibility for no arbitrage, is not a set of technologies whose impetus takes flight on the wings of the becoming-perfect of zero-arbitrage also the same dark angel who annihilates the pricing mechanism of finance capital?

But let us back up and away here from this obese epistemological aporia, and simply assert that it is equally interesting to reflect that Markowitz's insight was *also an ontological insight*, precisely in that if risk, in the end, proves not so much a property 'of' or 'in' any asset, per se, but rather constitutive of their interrelations, this means that risk itself is as plastic and nomadic as the other properties we have thus far considered. And once more our path of inquiry leads us to the thought that the financial asset *qua* economic object is in fact no object at all, or at least is only an object whose ex-centric objectivity is ever a moving horizon of extrinsically defined, dynamical economic properties.

iii. Our reader by now well knows our trope repeated throughout this essay – namely, that there are no properties inherently 'in' an asset, but such properties are (a) fleeting and (b) increasingly fungible; that (c) to witness the progressive differentiation of finance is to witness a progressive loosening of the time-honored invariance requirements on many a financial asset's economic properties; and so (d) when it comes to synthetic finance, we are now seeing a new (synthetic) kind of symmetry which differs in kind from that which actualizes between an asset and its image of value in either generic financial transactions or in classical exchange.

The question though here arises as to what, if any, are the limits to the fungibility of financial assets infused with the property of risk, when today we notice that rather than being gradually eliminated (e.g., through portfolio diversification, hedging with whole or partial objects, etc.), risk appears to have actually proliferated en masse?

Relatedly, if risk is contingent and plastic and obviously not endemic to any asset, does refracting an amount of risk present in a generic financial asset now through its synthetic incarnation do anything to change its substance – as we saw for instance, with both divisibility and reversibility?

Let us address these two questions in order: the first we address immediately below; the second we address in 'Cash Flow.' We wish to carry both of these concerns into our case study in Essay Two.

It is notable how developed and refined financial discourse on risk has become since Markowitz first introduced the world of finance to the notion that market risk has a particularity to it that is qualitatively different from nonsystematic or generalized risk, insofar as so many new types of risk are now perceived to have progressively differentiated themselves from out of his original binary distinction – and all of which have notably leapt from out of the Zeus' head of market risk, i.e., that contingent, volatile, and leftover risk which can neither be diversified-out of a portfolio nor completely hedged away.

Contemporary comparisons with Tobin are again illustrative of this change. Tobin tellingly speaks of the 'unpredictability' of assets, rather than of their risks. He informs his reader that it is possible to classify financial assets by those that are 'perfectly predictable,' those that are only 'partially predictable,' and those that are 'imperfectly predictable.'[33]

We need not dwell at length on Tobin's elaboration of this problematic distinction to grasp the main point to be taken from it herein: It is remarkable to see that Tobin feels comfortable defining for his reader an asset with perfect predictability – by which he means an asset lacking volatility, contingency, or otherwise absent any risk. And it is noteworthy that he gives as an example the generic financial asset of a US government bond. When Tobin notes that '[f]or a bond of the federal government, *there is almost by definition* no risk of default,' he is of course referring as much to the fact that, as he says, 'the currency in which the bond is payable is simply a different kind of obligation by the same government,' as he is '*by definition*' referring to the now thoroughly suspicious, and yet for financial modeling purposes, absolutely crucial concept of *the risk free rate*.[34]

iv. Let us stop here and assess the contemporary ontological significance of Tobin's 1960's citation of a paradigmatic example of the 'perfectly predictable' asset of a US government bond. Or rather, let us consider the contemporary 'risk free' status of its yield – which, because of its ostensible and relative stability, serves as a benchmark for the risk free rate; and thus is an essential variable for the modeling and actual pricing of money market and capital assets.

Malz, by comparison, devotes a section of his book to the concept of the risk free rate (Sec. 2.5 'Benchmark Interest Rates'), but apparently feels much less confident than Tobin does asserting that the risk free rate is indeed free of risk. In fact, when discussing the risk free rate, risk is actually all Malz sees:

> The term *risk-free rate* is something of a misnomer: there are no truly riskless returns in the real-world economy. The term is usually used to mean 'free of default risk.' There are two types of interest rates that are conventionally taken as proxies for a riskless return. Which of these types of risk-free rate is used depends on the context. In any case, we should be aware that these are conventions or benchmarks, used for pricing and analytics, but not to be taken as riskless returns.[35]

Malz proceeds to discuss the *interest rates attached to government bonds*, which he concedes 'are often considered riskless assets.'[36] But then he pauses to underscore to his reader (as if now raising his voice to be heard): '*This analysis, however, leaves out several risks*,' which he then goes on to identify and define as: default risk, interest rate risk, non-trivial credit risk, inflation risk, exchange rate risk, credit migration risk, to name just a few of the risks associated with this risk free rate.[37]

Malz then moves to discuss *money market rates*, which are short term interest rates on assets with a year or less on their maturity. Our reader may or may not know that at present the two most common standardized money market rates are: (i) those benchmarked at LIBOR (London Interbank Offered Rate) –which we now realize, from the 2008 (but disclosed only in 2012) LIBOR rate-fixing scandal, is permeated with fraud risk and other operational risks (of which Malz – whose book was published in 2011 – likely yet has no definitive knowledge), not to mention 'a significant degree' of credit risk, exchange rate risk, and so on. And also (ii) the *repo rate*, which is a benchmark rate for interbank repurchase agreements, and – as Lehman Bros. *et al.* during the 2008 financial crisis painfully experienced – itself is obviously not immune to either counterparty risk, or operational risks, such as fraud risk and other risks.

It is therefore not inconsequential for our consideration of the property of risk that these two proxies for the 'risk free rate' are increasingly less and less rates that we can meaningfully regard as free of risk. It is as if the 'real world risks' we label 'risk free rates,' ostensibly caged within our financial models, are constantly buzzing and shaking, trying to leap out from within them and back out into this world. And it is not inconsequential that back in the 1960s, this risk free rate was less problematically 'riskless' for Tobin.

Moreover, Malz can easily concede that there are no perfectly predictable assets, because for Malz there are no financial assets which lack the property of risk – there is always a leftover risk that is inherently unpredictable. Malz illustrates the mutant evolution of new species of risks proliferating from within but now also beyond simple market risk; he itemizes them in a Table near the front of his book – complete with definitions (which we shorthand) and a comprehensive list of sub-risks differentiating themselves from a variety of principal risks. They are:

i *market risk* (risk of market price fluctuation), which has (a) price risk, (b) execution risk, and (c) mark-to-market risk;
ii *credit risk* (risk of deterioration in the value of debt, or of creditworthiness), which has (a) default risk, (b) credit migration risk, (c) counterparty risk, and (d) clearing and settlement risk;
iii *liquidity risk* (risk of loss or deterioration of liquidity), which has (a) market liquidity risk, and (b) funding liquidity risk;
iv *model risk* (risk of incorrect models);
v *operational risk* (risk of policy and control breakdown);
vi *legal risk* (risk of enforceability or unenforceability of contractual obligations, or lawsuit), which has (a) fraud risk, (b) regulatory risk, and (c) compliance risk;
vii *reputational risk* (risk of bad publicity); and
viii *systemic risk* (risk of the cessation or serious impairment of system-wide circulation of debt).[38]

v. In our contemporary world of finance the night is dark with risk, indeed. However, that financial spaces of exchange constitute a world permeated through and through with risk is less a problem that, according to Malz, needs to be solved, than it is the way the pricing mechanism for financial assets works. And that different risks more than ever now circulate in the spaces of exchange of financial markets is far from incompatible with our ontological observation that risk – as a property – is contingent and plastic and always a mobile ground on which the shaky legs of price and value continuously seek to consummate their fickle union.

To be clear: it is not the case that the fungibility of financial assets is a characteristic that is utterly unaffected by the property of risk. But it is also the case that risk is a property that is just as pliable, just as isolable, and just as contingent as is any other property we have thus far considered. It is merely a matter of once again revising our understanding of what precisely materiality is, in order to observe that the risk – and in particular the risk embedded in maturity – which is the principal source of volatility, unpredictability, and so on in generic financial transactions, *is now in synthetic finance converted into a source of symmetry.*

No property of a financial asset better illustrates this fact than cash flow, a consideration of which will allow us to weave together the remaining threads of our analysis of the properties of financial assets we have discussed above.

Cash flow

i. What is the return on a financial asset? The answer to this question has nothing to do with the value of an asset, and everything to do with the property of cash flow. Or more specifically, the value of an asset has everything to do with the property of cash flow.

Cash flow is often defined to include all dividends paid on stock shares; interest paid on any debt, such as coupon payments or principal repayment on discounted bonds; and returns from the sale price of a financial asset or any other economic object relative to its purchase price – and especially the nominal return on an asset relative to its real return, i.e., its basic, unadjusted, expected dollar return versus its dollar return adjusted for loss of purchasing power, and as a result of inflation, etc. For all that, the matter of cash flow is quite simple.

ii. The auxiliary and ultimately contingent physicality shared by so many assets obtaining the property of cash flow should not distract us from its true materiality, or cause us to be misinformed about its basic material character: cash flow has no necessary connection to any particular financial asset, but rather is a property whose determination is wholly predicated on the space of its transformation in the course of exchange.

Habit and a deep-seated realist sentiment no doubt cause our expectation that where any phenomenon occurs it is necessarily connected to or in some way derived from a physical object. But as we have observed throughout, this naïve realism confuses the meaning of materiality, results in a bad ontology, and is the principal analytical culprit behind what we have disparaged as 'asset-fetishism.'

Perhaps other than Deleuze, no one was more critical of the bad ontology resulting in asset-fetishism than Fischer Black, whose essay 'Fundamentals of Liquidity' (1970) is to the ontology of finance what Black and Scholes's 'The Pricing Options and Corporate Liabilities' (1973) is to the epistemology of finance (though the former is obviously not as widely known as the latter). Herein Black makes a series of what initially appear to be rather counterintuitive claims, but which contain all the necessary observations to help us complete our opening attempt to revise our current political-economic concept of materiality.

Black commences his essay with the following assertion:

> In a world of equilibrium, it simply does not make sense to think of liquidity as a [property] of an asset that affects its expected return. There is no trade-off between liquidity and return.

A number of questions and concerns here immediately arise.

First, traditional methodological sentiments may incline us to wonder about the plausibility of the existence of a 'world of equilibrium' – i.e., of why we should care about something that happens 'in a world of equilibrium'? Or even accept that 'in a world of equilibrium' anything happens at all? Why does it matter, one will believe themselves to be critically inquiring, that it does or does not make sense to think of liquidity, let alone *any* such property as that which affects the cash flow of an asset, when in actuality we inhabit no such 'world of equilibrium'?

This may have once been a novel critique. But today we find this contention a bit sophomoric, not so much *wrong* as uninteresting – and at any rate it has now become worn-out through empty repetitions and its stand-alone use by those who lack a willingness to require their imagination to envision what our world is capable of becoming, but which it currently *in fact* is not. (And how can we ever take our institutions further than they presently go, when our own creative engineering is unwilling to step foot down the path capable of being prepared by imagination?)

Second, and more profoundly, we are struck by the blatant contradiction between, on the one hand Black's claim that there is no necessary connection between the property of liquidity and the cash flow of an asset, and on the other hand our Tobin-inspired definition of liquidity – which, as our reader will recall, is *the nominal relationship between maturity and value*. Is Black not making a wildly false claim – given our earlier definition of liquidity – when he says that liquidity and cash flow are unrelated? For if cash flow has value, and maturity is the temporal realization of value in a one-time or periodic form of cash flow, how can liquidity and cash flow be unrelated? Black's assertion does appear, at first glance, patently wrong.

It seems that a decision is required of the reader of 'Fundamentals of Liquidity.'

One reception to Black's aforementioned assertion is to simply dispense with its possibility outright. This is done either because we (a) assume that nothing actually happens in a world of equilibrium, since there is no world even capable of existing as such – which we apparently know with relative certainty if only because *it is a world which does not now exist*. Or we (b) notice the contradiction between our current understanding of liquidity, i.e., as a property which currently *does* have consequences for the realization of value, and in particular the value that actualizes in the form of cash flow, and which is ostensibly derived from an asset when that asset is transformed into its image of value as money in the course of an exchange; and then this contradiction, in turn, causes us to summarily reject the plausibility of Black's assertion of the independence of cash flow from liquidity.

However, there is yet another way of reading Black's assertion. If we are willing to temporarily indulge Black's assertion about the possible achievement of a world of equilibrium (or as we should prefer to think of it: as neither *strict equilibrium* nor *turbulence* (i.e., crisis), but rather as 'far-from-equilibrium'),[39] and if we are capable of thinking along with Black about the material consequences of 'the synthetic' for the property of liquidity (as well as the other economic properties we have thus far considered), we will see that in fact he is making a startling ontological forecast about the progressive differentiation of finance: namely, he is observing that the trajectory of synthetic finance signals an ontological movement towards hyperfungibility to the point of absolute non-differentiation between financial assets and their liquidity – which, if universally extended, in turn would mean a perfectly hedged world of exchange, a ubiquitous and incessant reversibility to all financial assets, a radical loosening of all invariance requirements on their properties, and consequently the realization of a world permanently far-from-equilibrium that would yet nonetheless amount to a kind of quasi-equilibrium!

In other words – and strange though it is to imagine – the extended logic of Black's projection would result in the actualization of a zero-arbitrage space of exchange, and therein an annihilation of the current pricing mechanism for financial assets. Indelicately put, this would signal the end of finance capitalism as we presently know it to be.

Black, of course, does not come right out and say this, which is why we have not simply reproduced, absent any commentary, the essay in its entirety for our reader; but rather, we have found it necessary to take up the task of unearthing the full consequences of his analysis herein. Let us consider the essential features of Black's nine-page essay, in order to see how he arrives at this implicit conclusion.

iii. First, it is important to observe that Black understands, as we do, that there are different classes of exchange which determine the differentiated properties and behavior of properties of an asset; and that this means that different kinds of assets may be grouped under their respective class of exchange.

This is crucial to understand: it opens-up our political-economic analysis to the study of the ontology of exchange, which we have already begun to pursue in Essay One herein; it allows us to pry deeper into a case study of synthetic finance, which we will pursue in Essay Two; and it provides us with a methodological foundation, in Essay Three, for developing a speculative materialist political economy whose wager is that of the monstrous, ex nihilo, ad infinitum power of the synthetic.

Let us consider the three classes of exchange.

Classical exchange

Historically, the earliest form of money-mediated exchange was *classical exchange*: this involves the exchange and immediate settlement of physical assets for their images of value as money.

Real assets can include any economic object with physical materiality, and whose quality and character of physicality is informative of its value, e.g., houses, horses, cars, and corn.

Because the time-horizon on the property of tenure of a classical exchange is restricted to immediate settlement, and while certainly not wholly exempt of kinds of risk (fraud, etc.), the cash flow connected to this class of exchange is relatively unaffected by volatility, for the image of value of the asset has little opportunity to depreciate over the course of the exchange.

Already in classical exchange there is *some albeit comparatively little fungibility* to the properties of its objects. Black observes, without mentioning by name, Marx's ontological division of the value of an asset into its use value and exchange value, to which we will return below. He says:

> A real [viz. physical] asset has two functions: it acts as a store of wealth [i.e., realized as and in exchange value], and it is an object that has value in use [i.e., use value]. In theory, these two functions can be separated, as when one person owns an asset, and another person rents it for use.[40]

The reason this is possible, i.e., the reason the asset can be repeated, or doubled, having both a use value that is virtual and real, and an exchange value that is actual and real, is because the classical object, to begin with, is a natural object. The classical object in 'its function' as an exchange value is the product of a repetition of the natural object that yet produces a new difference in kind: the natural object is repeated, and in the process of its repetition the classical object is actualized. For this reason in Essay Three we will turn to Deleuze's heterodox political economy, founded on the dynamical divergent evolutionary force of difference and repetition.

Generic finance

To begin with there was only classical exchange. Today, however, of course, there is also *generic finance* – the class of exchange of generic financial transactions: this involves the exchange of generic financial assets (Black simply dubs them 'financial assets'), and whose tenure is capable of having a number of time-horizons other than immediate settlement – which gives birth to the now differentiated property of maturity.

Like the reference classical objects make to natural objects, generic financial assets will often reference an economic object with physical materiality, and whose quality and character of physicality is usually if not always informative of its value, e.g., houses, horses, cars, and corn. But generic financial assets are non-physical economic objects, whose quality and character of physicality will generally *not* be informative of its value, e.g., loans, bonds, bills, and stock. For this reason we can see and say that the class of exchange of generic finance already includes within it the class of exchange of classical exchange. That is to say, *historically* classical exchange ostensibly precedes generic finance, but *ontologically* generic finance is seen to be the broader class of exchange, and is therefore more fundamental, more generalized, and more original than its apparent, usual, historical predecessor – for it always includes the latter within itself, but never vice versa.

When considering maturity we observed that in generic financial transactions the time-horizon of the tenure of the exchange is loosened beyond immediate settlement; but we did not then have the occasion to consider a number of important consequences that result for the other properties of the assets involved. First and foremost is that maturity and cash flow need now no longer be organized in linear sequence. Indeed, let us recall the subtle and basic but radical alteration to the character of tenure which we earlier observed was ushered in by the historical arrival of generic finance, and caused the property of maturity to differentiate itself from out of tenure. In classical exchange, tenure was always restricted to immediate settlement. But once the invariance requirement on the time-horizon of tenure is loosened, there is no longer any impediment to the properties of risk and cash flow from coming and going, or growing or shrinking – and so also there is no obstruction to their nonlinear sequential arrangement in the space of exchange.

It is precisely this new fungible character of maturity, and its subsequent ability to establish a nonlinear sequential relationship with cash flow, that allows Black to make the following observation:

> The fact that liquidity should not affect the return on investment in real assets becomes … clear when we consider the relation between the purchase or sale of an asset and the cash flow connected with the purchase or sale.
>
> There is virtually no relationship between the legal transaction in which a buyer agrees to pay a certain amount to a seller, in return for an asset owned by the seller or services to be provided by the seller, and the settlement of the transaction in the form of one or more cash flows.[41]

For this reason, Black observes that there is no endogenous constraint preventing, for instance, the seller of an asset from borrowing from another party the entirety of the cash flow he will receive from the sale of the asset prior to the commencement of the sale itself. Or the seller of the asset may choose to extend a line of credit to the buyer, and will thus receive periodic payments agreed to under the terms established at the commencement of the sale.

Therefore, Black observes, the seller can receive the cash flow from the sale either prior to, periodically during, or sometime well-after the sale itself (i.e., '[b]oth buyer and seller can arrange to have the actual cash flows occur at convenient times that bear almost no relationship to the time of the sale'). And this is only possible because in a generic financial transaction, cash flow is no longer predicated on any causal relation to liquidity, since the property of cash flow and maturity need not be organized in linear sequence.

Black then goes a step further. He observes that if it is the case that 'both the buyer and seller can arrange for the cash flow to occur at a future time that is fixed in advance,' and if the result is that 'both of them can know well in advance when the cash flow will occur,' then it is also the case that 'neither [of them] has the problem of dealing with unexpected cash flows.'[42]

In other words, Black is asserting that the now sequentially nonlinear capacity of the property of cash flow, and its ability to be effectively isolated as a property, and then mutably transferred in both time and space, and independent of the physicality of the asset itself, means that risk should be equally isolable from the asset, and thus capable of being completely hedged away by distributing it across the entirety of the space-time of the exchange.

However, even the least critically minded among us must give pause here. We know things are not as simple as this. In fact – and as we observed above (please see 'Risk') – not only is it the case that rarely, if at all, is any generic financial transaction free of risk, it turns out that even the 'risk free rate of return' is not a rate of return that is free of risk. Not only is it not the case that risk has not been eliminated or reduced whatsoever in generic financial transactions, it is more than ever the case that any generic financial transaction is always permeated through and through with often hidden and unexpected risks. And not only is cash flow in generic finance not immune to the risk embedded in maturity, rather it seems that cash flow is more so exposed to volatility than ever before.

And why? In short, simply because when the time-horizon on the tenure of exchange is extended beyond immediate settlement, the augmentation and differentiation of new kinds of risk now accompanying maturity are free to proliferate, and the image of value of the asset now has all the opportunity to randomly fluctuate over the newly extended time-horizon – which is an opportunity that in classical exchange it had previously lacked. Generic finance thus potentially has all the risks to which Malz alerts his reader (please see 'Risk'), e.g., wild fluctuations in the image of value, payment default risk, volatility risk, interest rate risk, inflation risk, currency risk, etc., yet with none of the prior certainty accompanying the strict invariance requirements on the economic properties governing a classical exchange.

Synthetic finance

How then does Black resolve his forecast for a world of equilibrium – in which liquidity is unrelated to cash flow – given the seemingly natural tendency of these new risks accompanying the property of maturity in generic financial transactions to now differentiate themselves, proliferate freely and en masse, and all the concrete consequences for possible fluctuations to the object's image of value, and subsequent effect on its cash flow?

Black replies by making an ontological observation about financial assets – an observation about another kind of exchange made possible by finance, and in a sense already embedded in it from the very beginning:

> Like a real asset, a financial asset may have more than one function. In addition to serving as a store of wealth, a financial asset makes it possible to transfer risk from one person to another, and may make it possible for speculators to make 'bets' on the fortune of a particular company.

But again, Black notes, just as with Marx's ontological division of the value of a physical asset into its use value and exchange value [namely, store of wealth], so too is the liquidity embedded in the exchange value of a financial asset ontologically isolable from its risk. For as Black notes:

> these [two] functions are separable. There is no reason why the person who supplies the money for a financial asset should take the risk associated with the asset. And the risk can be transferred from one person to another independently of any transfer of the money invested from one person to another.[43]

As an example, Black cites the generic financial asset of a long term corporate bond:

> There is no theoretical reason why a financial institution could not guarantee, for a fee, the payments of interest and principal on the bond. We would expect the fee to be related to the amount of market risk in the bond. Such a bond would then be, from an investor's point of view, virtually free of risk of default. The transfer of the bond would be completely independent of the transfer of the guarantee.
>
> Similarly, there is no theoretical reason why a financial institution should not guarantee a long term bond against fluctuations in price. This would convert the long term bond into a short term bond, from the holder's point of view, and would separate the function of supplying the money from the function of bearing the risk of price fluctuations.[44]

Of course, though perhaps in the 1970s these ideas were unique to Black, today we recognize that an exchange which involves the 'guarantee, for a fee, the payments of interest' on a bond is accomplished through the sale and purchase of the subclass of credit derivatives of an *interest rate swap* (IRS). Likewise, an exchange which involves the 'guarantee, for a fee, the payments of … principal' on a bond is accomplished through the sale and purchase of another subclass of credit derivatives, this time a *credit default swap* (CDS). And an exchange which involves the guarantee of a long term bond against fluctuations in price – and which converts this risk seemingly attached to the bond itself now into an eliminable property of that exchange – is accomplished through the sale and purchase of the subclass of credit derivatives broadly known as a *total rate of return swap* (TRS). Black here, in other words, is anticipating the proliferation of credit derivatives and various subclasses of assets belonging to synthetic finance.

Black further observes:

> A second institution might take over the guarantee function from the first institution, without affecting the bond holder. And the holder of the bond could sell it to another holder without any change in the institution guaranteeing the bond.
>
> It is clear that the risk of default on the bond, and changes in the fortunes of the issuer, will affect the terms on which the guarantee can be transferred. If there is a dealer in guarantees, these factors may affect his spreads. But these factors will not affect the terms on which the bond itself can be transferred. Nor will they affect the spreads of bond dealers.

And why will such factors neither affect the terms of transfer of the financial asset of the bond itself, nor the bid-ask spreads of the bond dealers – nor, for that matter, any operation costs which otherwise affect the amount of reversibility adhering to the generic financial asset of the long term bond over the course of the exchange? *In short, simply because the property of cash flow is independent of the actuality of the generic asset itself.* 'It is clear,' Black says, that any material change to interest rates '*will affect* the terms on which the guarantee' (i.e., the guarantee against the risk embedded in the maturity of the exchange) can be transferred – which is to say that the value, price, and cash flow connected to the synthetic asset itself *will be affected.* But that conversely, any material changes to interest rates *will not affect* the terms on which the generic financial asset of the bond itself is bought or sold.

And so the thought arises: if the price, value, and cash flow of the actuality of the generic asset (in this case, a bond) *is materially unaffected*, but the price, value, and cash flow of the synthetic asset *is affected*, we are unjustified to continue to assert that the former is in any important economic sense 'more material' than the latter. In fact, Black illustrates that precisely the opposite is true.

He observes the material consequences for the *divisibility* of such a financial asset.

> Thus a long term corporate bond could actually be sold to three separate persons. One would supply the money for the bond; one would bear the interest rate risk; and one would bear the risk of default.

He observes the material consequences for the *reversibility* of such a financial asset.

> The cost of transferring the bonds themselves, under these circumstances, would be nearly zero.

And he observes the material consequences for the *liquidity* and *cash flow* of such a financial asset, given that the *risk* in *maturity* is isolable and fungible (or 'transferable' is how he puts it).

> The two factors that are said to make an asset relatively illiquid, are risk and transfer costs. But we have seen that the risk of a financial asset is separable from the asset as a store of wealth, and that the transfer costs are associated with the risk of the asset rather than with the asset as a store of wealth.
>
> Thus liquidity in financial assets has nothing to do with cash flows. Cash transfers are completely independent of risk transfers, and liquidity, if it has any meaning at all, is associated with risk transfers rather than with cash transfers.

iv. Black truly is here in 1970 mapping the progressive fungibility of financial assets. As we have labored to observe throughout, Black presumes that the economic properties of an asset constitute its dynamic and plastic essence, rather than that there is some kind of inherent 'being' to an asset, from which its properties derive their nature.

In fact, our reader will see that Black is really just unearthing the material consequences of the fungible and contingent character of economic properties, as such: if moneyness, divisibility, reversibility, liquidity, maturity, risk, and cash flow are isolable and not inherent to an asset, the first conclusion is that the extensive actuality of the asset does not matter in the least, *materially* speaking. This means that we must further examine the *intensive* properties of assets. And second, we are then presented with a picture of, and must further inquire into the significance that, financial assets, or rather their properties –whose becoming is constitutive of their ostensible objectivity – are increasingly so fungible?

This is to ask, what are the broader material consequences for our financial system as we witness the progressive differentiation of a class of exchange whose invariance requirements on the economic properties of assets are ever more so loosened, in which the properties of assets are ever more so mobile, plastic, and hyperfungible?

Black provides us with one answer, when he foreshadows a (post-finance capitalist) 'world of equilibrium':

> [In such a world] a person or institution does not need to hold liquid assets to help handle unexpected cash flows. Almost all cash flows are expected, and the cost and risk associated with handling those cash flows that are unexpected are very low.

First ontological principle of synthetic finance

i. We have begun to realize that there are some profound ontological consequences to draw from the fact that any given generic financial asset is capable of being divided among its constitutive economic properties, and that risk and cash flow are therefore especially isolable from any given generic financial asset.

For again, if, as we have observed throughout, the objectivity of the asset is merely a retroactively posited meeting ground for the fleeting and always temporary clearing in the woods of the market for economic properties to collect and congeal into this vacant property called *value*, then it seems we have arrived at a first ontological principle about the character of synthetic finance – and which we will credit Black for implicitly drawing our attention to herein.

Namely, if risk is connected to cash flow, but not necessarily liquidity; and if there is no endogenous limitation on the ability to transfer risk by synthetically creating its portal ex nihilo and ad infinitum; consequently, so too there are absolutely no endogenous limitations to the distribution of cash flow whatsoever. This is the first ontological principle of our speculative materialism. This is the first ontological principle of synthetic finance. The significance of its meaning must now be further established.

Notes

1 James Tobin, 'Properties of Assets,' in *Money, Credit, and Capital*, McGraw Hill, 1981.
2 Allan Malz, *Financial Risk Management: Models, History, and Institutions*, Wiley, 2011 p. 424.

3 This is also more or less Perry Mehrling's account of the crisis, outlined in his book, *The New Lombard Street: How The Fed Became the Dealer of Last Resort*, Princeton University Press, 2011.

4 Tobin p. 15.

5 This is an issue for further ontological examination in the forthcoming book, *Infinite Leverage*. For now, we will note that Prigogine and Nicolis, for example, have observed that

> '[a] striking difference between linear and nonlinear [systems] is whether the property of superposition holds or breaks down. In a linear system the ultimate effect of the combined action of two different causes is merely the superposition of the effects of each of the causes taken individually. But in a nonlinear system adding a small cause to one that is already present can induce dramatic effects that have no common measure with the amplitude of the cause.'
>
> G. Nicolis and I. Prigogine, *Exploring Complexity: An Introduction*, W.H. Freeman & Co., 1989

The notion of superposition's nonapplicability in nonlinear phenomena comingles with Deleuze's point that in qualitative multiplicities there is no necessary exact correspondence between number and unit, quantity and magnitude, division and amount. If, as we have good reason to believe (and will demonstrate in Essay Three) synthetic financial assets are qualitative multiplicities, we must further examine the nonlinear and potentially radical nonadditive capacities of synthetic finance. For more on nonadditive causality, also see Mario Bunge, *Causality and Modern Science*, Harvard University Press, 1959, chapter 6.

6 Tobin p. 15.

7 For example, see Oliver Suess, Carolyn Bandel, and Kevin Crowley, 'Death Derivatives Emerge from Pension Risks of Living Too Long,' *Bloomberg News*, May 16, 2011.

8 Malz, in a striking contrast to Tobin, alludes to the increased reversibility of financial assets which had previously been relatively lacking such property, when sketching some concrete effects of innovations in financial technologies on the invariance requirements marking generic finance. For example, he observes:

> The wave of innovation began at a relatively slow pace in the 1960s in the money markets, with the introduction of negotiable certificates of deposit (CDs). There had long been time-deposits, bank deposits repaid to the depositor at the end of a fixed interval rather than on demand, *but negotiable CDs could be sold prior to maturity at a market-adjusted interest rate in the secondary market, rather than bought at a cost.*'
>
> Malz p. 5 (my emphasis)

The commoditization of deposits to be bought and sold in money markets, and the subsequent differentiation of the property of reversibility in what was the previously irreversible financial asset of a time-deposit, but now marking the negotiable CD, is consistent with a general trend of the increasing plasticity and fungibility of financial assets, whose ontological significance for our broader financial system should not be underemphasized.

9 As if directly observing the progressive differentiation of the system of markets of finance, and in particular the development of a class of exchange of synthetic finance from out of the class of exchange of generic finance, Deleuze notes: 'in the infinite movement of degraded likeness from copy to copy, we reach a point at which everything changes nature, at which copies flip over into simulacra and at which, finally, resemblance or spiritual imitation gives way to repetition.' Gilles Deleuze, *Difference & Repetition*, Columbia University Press, 1996, p. 128.

10 Jean Laplanche, 'The Unfinished Copernican Revolution,' in *Essays on Otherness*, Routledge, 1999.
11 F. Fabozzi, F. Modigliani, and F. Jones, *Foundations of Financial Markets and Institutions*, Pearson, 2009, p. 174.
12 Tobin p. 12.
13 Ibid. p. 12.
14 *International Accounting Standards*, IAS 7. Statement of Cash Flows, 1992.
15 Tobin p. 12.
16 Ibid. p. 13.
17 Ibid. p. 13.
18 Ibid. p. 13.
19 Ibid. p. 13.
20 On becoming, see G. Deleuze and F. Guattari, *A Thousand Plateaus: Capitalism & Schizophrenia*, University of Minnesota Press, 1987, esp. Chapter 10.
21 As to how an asset, when graduating from the highly illiquid, metamorphosizes into irreversibility, rather than moving on to absolute or pure illiquidity, Tobin explains:

> [T]here is no complete illiquidity to place at the opposite pole from perfect liquidity. If nothing can be realized from the disposition of an asset at a given moment no matter how careful and how long the preparation, the definitions say that it has no value at this time; its liquidity therefore is indeterminate, although such an asset is illiquid in the everyday usage of this term. An asset may have zero value today but positive value in the future, anticipated with more or less certainty; and an asset of zero value to its owner today may cost much more than zero to acquire. Both points are illustrated by the rights of a participant in a retirement program before he is eligible for its benefits. Such assets will be termed completely irreversible rather than illiquid.
>
> Tobin p. 13

22 Ibid. p. 14.
23 Ibid. p. 14.
24 Fritz Heichelheim, *An Ancient Economic History: From the Palaeolithic Age to the Migrations of the Germanic, Slavic, and Arabic Nations (Volume I)*, A.W. Sijthoff-Leyden, 1965, p. 53.
25 Ibid. p. 53.
26 Ibid. pp. 53–54.
27 Ibid. p. 22.
28 Ibid. p. 54.
29 Fabozzi *et al.* p. 173.
30 Tobin p. 12.
31 Malz p. 461.
32 We earlier observed in passing that ETFs (exchange-traded funds) are a technology for engineering increased divisibility into financial assets, and that one effect of the proliferation of ETFs is that there is now no apparent endogenous limit to the divisibility of any financial asset; this is a clear loosening of the invariance requirement on the denomination-size of a financial asset, which could be taken down to a penny or lower. However, it is also worth noting that another property whose invariance requirement is progressively loosened with the ETF is maturity – which is its sub-property of delay-time. Malz alludes to the relaxed invariance requirements on the delay-time of index funds in the ETF, which is more restrictive in a traditional mutual fund ('An ETF tracks a well-defined index, like many mutual funds, *but can be traded intraday, in contrast to a mutual fund, which can only trade at its end of day net asset value* (NAV).' Malz p. 6 (my emphasis)).
33 Tobin p. 16.
34 Ibid. p. 16.

35 Malz p. 88.
36 Ibid. p. 88.
37 Ibid. p. 89.
38 Ibid. pp. 35–39.
39 See G. Nicolis and I. Prigogine, *Exploring Complexity: An Introduction*, W.H. Freeman & Co.
40 Fischer Black, 'Fundamentals of Liquidity' (unpublished) p. 1.
41 Ibid. p. 3.
42 Ibid. pp. 3–4.
43 Ibid. p. 4.
44 Ibid. p. 4, 5.

2 The materialism of synthetic finance

A case study on credit derivatives in seven notes

Note 1 Credit default swaps

i. When, as political economists, we encounter credit derivatives and other synthetic financial objects, we must not overlook that their progressive differentiation from generic finance signals an important phase transition in our dynamical system of economic institutions, with deep historical-materialist significance.

Brief consideration of the ontology of a single-name credit default swap (CDS) already illustrates this truth.

A CDS is a bilateral exchange between two parties – one of whom is called the protection buyer, the other is called the protection seller. The terms of exchange of the CDS make reference to a certain notional value, which is the payment obligation of a reference entity. The protection buyer pays the protection seller a cash premium on a quarterly, annual, daily, or any other agreed-to periodic basis. In return, the seller agrees to make protection payment to the buyer upon occurrence of a credit event in the reference entity (Figure 2.1).[1] The object of this exchange is therefore called a credit default swap, because the parties to the exchange are *swapping* the risk of a *default* or some like-credit event on a *credit/debt* obligation.

Someone or something somewhere owes someone or something else money. This debt obligation comprises the reference obligation of the reference entity: there has been some preceding generic financial exchange of some generic financial asset (i.e., a mortgage, a bond, or some other debt asset), whose event risk and cash flow the CDS replicates. However, while the CDS makes reference to this generic financial asset, its value, and the single-name of the obligor party to the generic financial exchange, the parties to the CDS may be (and usually are) otherwise independent of and unrelated to the generic financial exchange. For this reason the exchange is 'synthetic.' We call the exchange of credit derivatives – in this case the exchange of a CDS – a 'synthetic financial exchange' because the exchange involves a synthetic swapping of the risk and cash flow of a reference entity, derived from a generic financial exchange, but to which neither party to the synthetic exchange need be party to begin with.

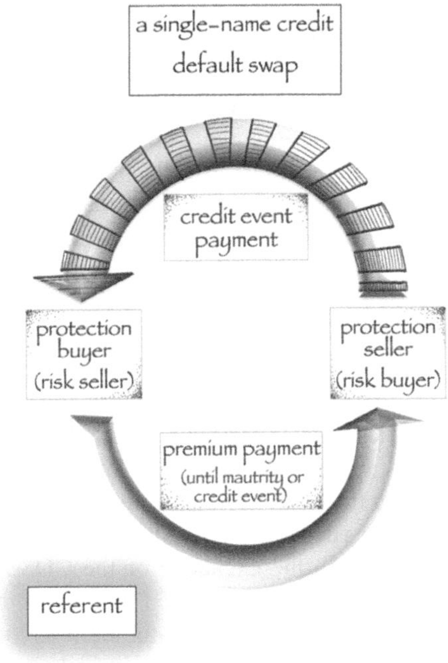

Figure 2.1 Single-name credit default swap.

ii. We have provided an elementary description of a single-name CDS commonly found in any literature on credit derivatives, so let us consider its elementary material significance.

We have observed that this kind of exchange is called 'synthetic' insofar as neither party to the exchange is required to have original exposure in the generic financial exchange, whose asset comprises the reference obligation from which the synthetic financial exchange of the CDS is derived, and on which to begin with the entirety of the CDS transaction is ostensibly predicated. Therefore, when attending to the process of 'synthetic replication' of a generic financial asset, we should observe that the CDS is an economic object to be exchanged like any other, but only insofar as it is a process: a credit default swap is both an economic object (namely, an asset, a commoditized object) and a process (namely, a technology) for the synthetic replication of a generic financial asset; it is the constitutive process of the exchange that actualizes the synthetic asset, as such, rather than the exchange constituting an exchange of some preexisting, pre-actualized asset.

However, unlike any other economic object, there is no inherent limit on its capacity to replicate and distribute itself ad infinitum. Comparison with the other two classes of exchange quickly reveals why this is the case:

- In a *classical exchange*, which is comprised of physical objects, a specific coat requires a certain amount of cloth, whose availability places physical limitation on the number of coats in circulation.
- So too in a *generic financial exchange*, which is comprised of generic financial assets, the financial asset of, for instance a mortgage, correlates to the physical object of the house; and the loan-to-value ratio of any mortgage is necessarily bound by its correlation to the house as a physical structure.
- In a *synthetic financial exchange*, by contrast it is enough that: (a) only *one* coat, or *one* house, or *one* mortgage exists; so that (b) the economic properties of risk and cash flow otherwise linked to that asset (i.e., the one coat, one house, or one mortgage) can be synthetically replicated *ex nihilo* and *ad infinitum*; in order to (c) create a new asset in itself – which is the synthetic financial asset.

iii. When we say, then, that the parties to the CDS have 'swapped' the risk of default on the obligation of a reference entity, we are observing that they have synthetically exchanged a risk and cash flow otherwise adhering to a generic financial asset, i.e., as two economic properties otherwise attached to the generic asset. But let us keep in mind that prior to the exchange of the CDS, neither party to this synthetic exchange need be originally exposed to any risk or cash flow connected to the referent. Ownership-of, or exposure-to, the referent is not a requirement for transacting a synthetic financial exchange – which means that neither the protection seller nor protection buyer need be the obligor, or creditor, in the preexisting generic financial exchange. But to the extent that the protection buyer and seller transact a CDS, they *have* created a new asset, and this asset does have the very real material economic properties of risk and cash flow.

In this respect, we will observe that the act of synthetic exchange effectively creates – synthetically, yes, but no less in reality – a risk and cash flow which did not exist before. There is no transfer of private property, no concrete production by labor of any classical economic object, and whose intrinsic value is supposedly congealed therein, nor any new generic financial asset or reference obligation. And yet, through the process of synthetic exchange, because there has occurred a new and ex nihilo proliferation of the economic properties of risk and cash flow, we cannot meaningfully deny that a synthetic exchange is any less an exchange, or lacking in profound material consequences.

In fact, the peculiar materiality of the synthetic financial asset now raises the important question of whether it is either the case that we need to liberalize our prior understanding of materiality, or even that the actualization of synthetic finance already radicalizes the very concept of materiality itself? This is an issue for further examination by speculative materialism.

Note 2 Total return swaps

i. We commenced Note 1 by asserting that the progressive differentiation of synthetic finance from generic finance signals an important phase transition in our dynamical system of economic institutions, with deep historical, materialist significance. And we briefly considered the ontology of a single-name CDS to inaugurate our illustration of this truth. Another type of credit derivative called a total return swap (TRS) is more revelatory, still.

A TRS is a bilateral exchange between two parties – (a) a protection buyer, who periodically transfers or 'swaps' the 'actual returns' from some reference asset or index of assets to (b) a protection seller, who in return transfers the 'total returns' of some agreed-to amount, calculated at a certain spread over or below a benchmarked base rate of return.

On the one hand, cash flow from the actual returns derives from its synthetic replication of the returns and current market value of a generic financial asset or index of assets: this includes replicating any discounts or coupons, and ongoing market appreciation/depreciation in the value of the generic referent. On the other hand, cash flow from the total returns is tethered to a base rate – e.g., LIBOR + X bps – agreed to by the parties to the TRS ahead of time (Figure 2.2).[2] This means that cash flows from the total returns and the actual returns are both ostensibly derived from the returns and current market value of the same generic referent, since the total returns is a reflection of the spread between the actual returns, less the benchmarked base rate of return.

For example, if the parties to the contract agree that the base rate for the total returns is to be LIBOR + X bps, the protection buyer is agreeing to swap with the protection seller the actual returns from a generic reference asset or assets – e.g., a corporate bond, or index of corporate bonds – in return for LIBOR + X bps. But if, for instance, there is any depreciation in the market value of the referent at some point during the tenure of the swap, the protection seller will transfer to the protection buyer the new difference between its actual returns and the total returns of the base rate spread. Likewise, in the event of any appreciation in value of the generic asset, the protection buyer will increase the payment of actual returns to the protection seller to reflect this change as well.

For this reason, sometimes the protection buyer is more precisely called the 'total return payer,' and the protection seller 'the total return receiver,' since the intention of the parties to the exchange is not so much the buying and selling of protection on a credit event, but the swapping of total valuation risks and cash flows attached to the respective referent. The object of this exchange is therefore called a 'total return swap' because the parties to the exchange are *swapping* the *total* risks determinate of the cash flow *return* on some generic financial asset or index of assets. And as with any credit derivative, the exchange is said to be 'synthetic' insofar as the exchange is synthetically replicating certain specified economic properties from its referent – in the case of a TRS, these properties are the total risks and cash flow, reflected as the total returns and ongoing market value of the generic financial asset or assets.

ii. Brief comparison of the ontologies of a single-name CDS and a single-name TRS will yield more insight.

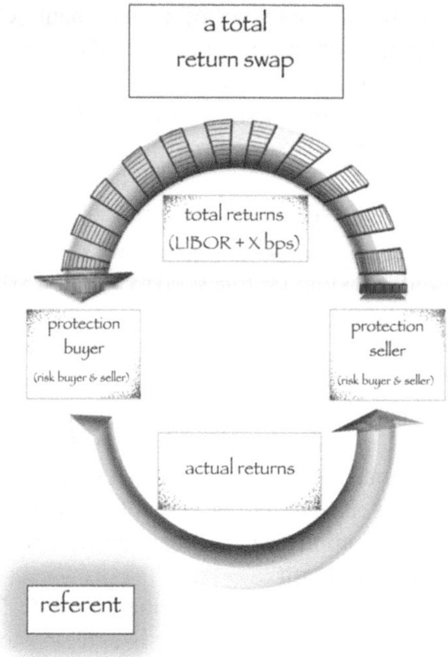

Figure 2.2 Total return swap.

First, in a TRS, the parties swap cash flows on an ongoing basis, and constantly adjust the amount to reflect any change in returns or market valuation of the referent; whereas in a CDS the payoff for the buyer is contingent upon the occurrence of a credit event. While in both cases there is nothing to prevent the occurrence of a credit event resulting in either cash or physical settlement and subsequent termination of the swap, it is worth observing that an adjustment in cash flow in the single-name CDS transaction is contingent upon a one-time credit event, while the TRS could be perpetually revalued on an ongoing basis, but written to include credit events as well. In this respect, the TRS already points towards the development of a structured synthetic financial asset – such as a synthetic CDO – whose cash flow is interminable, perpetually adjusted on an ongoing basis, and wherein the cash flow actually *is* the asset, as such. We will later indulge the question of what would be the concrete effects of universally distributing such a class of instruments.

Second, while a single-name CDS replicates exposure to an individual and specific reference obligation from a generic financial exchange, and notably does so through the act of exchanging a specific kind of risk – the risk of default, ratings downgrade, or some like-credit event; by contrast a single-name TRS replicates exposure to the *total* risks of an asset – including its default risk, interest rate risk, currency risk, etc. – and in this respect is a more comprehensive replication of the risks attaching to the generic referent. In fact, if the CDS definitions of a credit event were broadened so as to include any incremental change in cash flow or ongoing mark-to-market valuation of its referent, and if the requirement to terminate the swap with the occurrence of a credit event was simply dropped from the terms of the exchange (i.e., so that the swapped cash flow was perpetual and interminable), all other superficial ontological differences between a CDS and TRS would collapse. This is obviously not the case. But it does give us some insight into the progressive fungibility of synthetic financial objects which are otherwise lacking in either physical economic objects or in generic financial objects. And again, although we colloquially speak here of synthetic 'objects,' let us observe that – as with a CDS, so too with a TRS – it is the *process* of the exchange itself which constitutes the asset, rather than the exchange constituting the process by which some preexisting assets are exchanged.

And so finally, let us once more observe that in both instances of synthetic financial exchange thus far considered, the physical property ostensibly tied to the generic referent remains unaffected and otherwise untransformed; ownership of any physical assets remains totally unchanged, and so on. And yet in a synthetic exchange, the important economic properties of risk and cash flow are capable of being created ex nihilo, and plastically redirected or otherwise distributed. This plastic distributive potential of credit derivatives is a topic for further investigation by speculative materialism.

Note 3 Credit derivatives

i. We have begun to see that credit derivatives are a type of synthetic financial object capable of creating or destroying, extracting or injecting, distributing and redistributing a variety of risks and cash flows. As such, they are also a process by which the economic properties of risk and cash flow are synthetically created or destroyed, extracted or injected, distributed and redistributed to the parties of the exchange.

The counterparty in a synthetic financial exchange could be specific market participants – such as a hedge fund, bank, pension fund, and so on; or through the process of structured finance could be the capital markets more broadly. However, there is no technical impediment to the counterparty either being a horizontally organized set of nomadic groups, the State, or even some instrument for universality which would render the State, as such, obsolete. It is in fact very possible that the historical-materialist trajectory of synthetic finance points in this very direction.

Counterparties to a credit derivatives exchange are purchasing the economic properties of risk and associated cash flow. In this respect, single-name credit derivatives are a technology for exchanging the risk and cash flow attached to some generic financial asset, the latter of which in turn is in some way virtually connected to some physical object, or what we call a 'classical object,' e.g., as a house *qua* physical referent is to a mortgage *qua* generic financial referent, and so on. And yet we have repeatedly observed that, as with any synthetic exchange, all this occurs without *actually* exchanging either the generic financial asset or the classical object to which it is ostensibly linked, and which acts as the referent to the (synthetic) exchange. It is therefore no overstatement to say that with the advent of credit derivatives we see the ruse of private property laid bare: if a cash flow is capable of being traded without the physicality of the object changing parties, or being moved about in space or transformed whatsoever, it is because the intrinsic essence of any economic object *is* its exogenously effected heterogeneous mess of economic properties, n-dimensionally determined, and which are not essential or intrinsic to it. So if the truth of any exchange is its objectivity as capital, and whose materiality is ultimately defined by its cash flow, synthetic exchange illustrates the wholly inobjective nature of the asset, insofar as the asset qua object just 'happens to be there' as an extrinsic manifestation of the process of the exchange. Insofar as any economic object *is* its total set of economic properties, when such objects are in process by way of synthetic financial exchange, such properties are mobile, plastic, and fungible, i.e., capable of being created or destroyed, extracted or injected, distributed and redistributed elsewhere.

For this reason, in Notes 1 and 2 we commenced our illustration that the progressive differentiation of synthetic finance from out of generic finance signals an important phase transition in our dynamical system of economic institutions, with deep historical-materialist significance. In large part, vindication of this assertion is predicated on *the progressive fungibility of synthetic symmetry* – whose ontological significance will demand a more in-depth examination.

Presently, let us consider two elementary concrete examples to solidify our foundational understanding of credit derivatives, as we begin to deepen our understanding of this aforementioned truth.

ii. Our first example is that of a single-name CDS.

> Let us say that PB has purchased a senior secured bond issued by Marx Corp., whose notional value is $75 million, payable after 10 years. PB seeks to lessen, or hedge, its risk exposure to Marx Corp. (since PB has become increasingly anxious that the latter has trouble completing projects). PB thus enters into a CDS with PS. The notional value of the CDS is $50 million, with Marx Corp. as the reference entity, and senior unsecured bonds as the reference obligation (the referent). The terms of the CDS contract obligate PB to pay a protection premium of 75 bps to PS over the tenure of the contract, which is five years. According to the terms agreed to in the contract, settlement may be physical delivery or in cash.

Let us consider some basic material features of the asset convoked into being by this synthetic financial exchange.

To begin with, we have stated at the outset that PB is transacting the CDS for hedging purposes, insofar as PB owns the reference asset – which is the generic financial asset of a senior secured bond of Marx Corp. But this need not have been the case; PB could have just as readily transacted the same swap without owning the debt obligation of the Marx Corp. bond, since the requirement placed by the other two classes of exchange (i.e., classical exchange and generic financial exchange) on the unity of risk and physical possession is altogether dropped from a synthetic financial exchange. That is to say – and importantly – there has still been an acknowledgment of commensurability, equivalence, or *symmetry* between the synthetic object and its image of value as money – since symmetry is a necessary feature of *any* exchange, whether of classical objects, generic financial objects, or synthetic financial objects (indeed, lacking symmetry, no price will be agreed to, no exchange will occur). And yet we see that unlike in either a classical exchange or generic financial exchange, there is no necessary conjoining of actual risk exposure to a referent and physical ownership of the referent. For this reason we will say that in a CDS – as in any synthetic financial exchange – there is no required *collinearity of risk and physical ownership*. This also gives further meaning to our earlier assertion that with the advent of credit derivatives we are either witnessing the progressive abolition of private property, or if it still has any relevance to this class of exchange at all, it should be exclusively defined by substance of its risk and cash flow.

Along this same line of thought, our careful reader will have also become aware that, in the example above, there are a number of other basic ontological differences between the generic financial asset (of the Marx Corp. bond) and that of the synthetic asset (of the CDS). For instance, the actual bond held by PS has a maturity of ten years, its notional value is $75 million, and it is a senior secured bond. However, by contrast the tenure of the CDS has a maturity of five years, its notional value is $50 million, and its referent obligation is a senior unsecured bond. For this reason we will observe that in synthetic financial exchange, in this case a single-name CDS, a number of restrictions, or 'invariance requirements,' placed on the economic properties of the object in the other two classes of exchange are loosened or altogether dropped. The material significance of this is something we must examine in more depth. Such loosened invariance requirements marking synthetic exchange illustrates for us both the progressive fungibility of synthetic finance over the two other classes of exchange, as well as its natural proclivity for more radical usages.

Let us then briefly dwell on these loosened invariance requirements.

For example:

a As we observed above, there is no invariance requirement on *collinearity of risk and propriety*: e.g., the holder of the synthetically replicated risk and its cash flow from the generic referent is not required to be owner of or otherwise proprietarily exposed to the generic referent.

b There is no invariance requirement on *collinearity of tenures*: e.g., the generic referent has a ten year maturity, but its synthetic replica has a 5 year maturity.

c There is no invariance requirement on *collinearity of notional values*: e.g., the generic asset is for \$75 million, but the synthetic asset is for \$50 million.
d There is no invariance requirement on *collinearity 'in-kind'*: e.g., the generic financial asset is a senior secured bond, but the synthetically replicated asset is a senior unsecured bond.

We must further examine the ontological significance of this progressive relaxation on the collinearites present in the other two classes of exchange. What, if any, is the historical meaning of this progressive loosening of invariance requirements concomitant with the differentiation of synthetic finance as a class of exchange? However, for now, to begin with, it is enough that our reader recognizes that the required symmetry – i.e., between the economic object and its image of value as money – on which *any act of exchange* is predicated are nonetheless still achieved, while yet the invariance requirements on the economic properties of the object placed by classical exchange and generic financial exchange are loosened herein.

This means at least two things. First, it means that there are quantitatively different amounts of symmetry in each of the respective classes of exchange – classical, generic, and synthetic. For if, following the group theorists, symmetry is (a) defined as 'invariance to change,' and (b) measured by the number of the transformations that leave a property of an object or process invariant to change, then the fact that different classes of exchange have different invariance requirements on their respective economic properties means that, in turn, different amounts of symmetry mark the different acts of exchange; and these different acts of exchange can be grouped into different classes of exchange. Second, then, for this reason we know that insofar as synthetic finance as a class of exchange has the least restricted invariance requirements, this means that it has more symmetry than either of the other two classes of exchange from which it has historically differentiated itself. We must deepen our examination of the ontological importance of these truths as we proceed.

iii. Our second example is that of a TRS.

> Let us say that P has purchased, and is therefore generically invested in, an unsecured bond issued by Black Corp., which pays a fixed coupon of 7%. P enters into a TRS with R, in which P swaps the actual returns from the Black Corp. bond for the agreed-to spread of LIBOR + 100 bps. This means that under the terms of the contract, P will redistribute to R the actual coupon payments made by the Black Corp., plus or less any change in the market value of the bond. And in return, R agrees to pay P LIBOR + 100 bps.

Let us consider some basic features of this synthetic financial asset, which is best accomplished by reflecting on the material impact of the TRS for the parties involved.

For instance, for P: while on the one hand and superficially it is the case that P has *actually* invested in the generic financial asset of a bond issued by Black Corp., on the other hand it is also the case that P is now no longer *materially* invested in the generic financial asset of a bond issued by Black Corp. And why? Simply, by entering a TRS with R, P has now detached the economic property of risk from that bond, and sold off that risk to R, i.e., P has materially detached the risk from the generic financial asset by process of synthetic exchange, and redistributed that risk and its cash flow to R.

Conversely, for R: on the one hand and superficially R has not *actually* invested in the generic financial asset of the Black Corp. bond; but on the other hand by entering into the swap with P, it is also the case that R has purchased from P the risk in the Black Corp. bond – paying to P the purchase premium of LIBOR+100 bps, and receiving from P the actual returns from the Black Corp. bond – yet without physically owning the generic referent of the Black Corp. bond itself.

From this we can observe that, in this case, the synthetic financial exchange of a TRS equates to an exchange between P and R of the total risks and associated cash flow endemic to holding the Black Corp. bond, which are then redistributed in kind between the two parties. P retains as private property the generic asset of the bond, redistributing its actual returns to R. And while technically speaking R has not invested in and can otherwise claim no property ownership of the Black Corp. bond, nonetheless R does receive its actual returns, in turn agreeing to pay P the difference between the base rate spread and the actual returns. And finally, Black Corp. remains unaffected by the TRS in any way.

iv. Let us pause to briefly summarize both the *material significance* and *significance for materialism* of what we have thus far considered about synthetic finance, prior to further deepening our examination of its ontology.

We have so far really only made one point, but with a twofold-tiered exposition.

First, we observed in our example of the CDS that a synthetic asset replicates the generic financial asset from which it is ostensibly derived, but in the process loosens a number of invariance requirements on the economic properties that constitute the assets involved in the exchange – and which it is important to note *are* invariance requirements on the economic properties of the respective objects exchanged in the other two classes of exchange of classical exchange and generic finance. Therefore, while our common terminology often colloquially denotes the ontological status of the synthetic object as some kind of 'copy' or 'simulation,' a 'replica' that is always 'derived' from some 'underlier' – the latter of which is the generic referent acting as the 'model' for its 'copy,' and is therefore always perceived to somehow be a more 'real' object than its synthetic counterpart – we are increasingly seeing that things are not so simple as this. In fact, that there are far fewer invariance requirements as conditions for the achievement of symmetry in a synthetic exchange means that not only are the economic properties constituting such synthetic assets more pliable and fungible, but now we are also seeing that synthetic finance, as a class of exchange, has more symmetry than the other two classes of exchange from out of which it has historically differentiated itself. It turns out that synthetic objects are not so much 'less real' or have 'less reality' than other non-synthetic economic objects; rather, they have just as much reality, albeit it is of an apparently different ontological register. For this reason we will later examine why Deleuze says that of the three registers of reality – potentiality, actuality, and virtuality – the synthetic asset still partially belongs to the latter, which is every bit as 'real' as the actual, albeit ontologically different in kind.

Second, we observed in our example of the TRS that while a superficial understanding of credit derivatives may lend some cause for belief that synthetic finance – because its assets are temporally and *linearly* 'derived' from a generic referent – is an ontological subset of generic finance, once again we see that things are not as straightforward as one might expect. For already in our example of a single-name TRS, we saw that not only is it *not* the case that the causality of the generic financial asset is unidirectional on the synthetic asset, but now we see that a virtual causality from a synthetic exchange can be every bit as performative, material, and have very real material consequences on either a past (namely, preexisting) or even a future generic financial exchange. This means that the temporal causality of the synthetic exchange on the generic exchange can be either linear or nonlinear – which is once more illustrative of the fungibility of synthetic finance. If the referent from a generic financial exchange appears to act as the underlying model to be copied by the synthetic asset, but then the performative impact of the synthetic exchange retroactively redefines the material terms of its underlier, how can we meaningfully speak of one or the other object as having 'more reality,' when both sets of objects are constantly feeding into one another, and exogenously remaking each other's interiority?

This twofold peculiarity requires a more in-depth investigation into the ontology of synthetic finance – as a class of exchange that has differentiated itself from the other two classes of exchange, as a set of markets, the objects populating those markets, and in turn their constitutive mobile, fungible, and dynamical economic properties. This a future task for speculative materialism.

Note 4 Tranches

i. Hitherto our consideration of credit derivatives has concerned single-named assets. We considered a single-name CDS and a single-name TRS, both of which were synthetic assets replicating a single-name referent (a corporate bond) from a single-name reference entity (a corporation). However, the deep historical-materialist significance of synthetic finance concerns the differentiation of multi-name credit derivatives (sometimes also called 'portfolio swaps' or 'portfolio credit derivatives') from out of their single-name incarnation – and in particular their usage, when combined with the technology of securitization, to engineer *structured synthetic financial assets*. For this reason, we will expand our understanding of the peculiar but profound materiality of synthetic finance by now turning our discussion to securitization, or structured finance.

We will inaugurate this discussion by examining tranches.

While single-name credit derivatives make reference to a single obligation (e.g., a bond) of a single entity (e.g., Marx Corp. or Black Corp.), multi-name credit derivatives reference a pool of obligations from a pool of names.

From one perspective, multi-name credit derivatives are simply the composition of a series of single-name credit derivatives into one portfolio. However, this only tells half of the story. The radical transformational essence of structured finance is its capacity – as a technology, a process, an object, and method of synthetic exchange – to aggregate a multi-named set of heterogeneous risks into one homogenous pool with a single risk, and then re-segregate this risk into different classes, whereby the risks and cash flows ontologically change in kind in the course of being structured as such. These new classes are called 'tranches,' which may be arranged in a variety of ways, to obtain a variety of specified risks and their associated cash flows.

Therefore, 'structured finance' is the term we use to define a process for the de-differentiation and subsequent re-differentiation of the economic property of risk by method of tranching: it is a process for the pooling and redistribution of risk, through which any risks and cash flows (as well as other economic properties) become not only fungible, plastic, mobile, and substitutable, but now also capable of dynamically changing in kind.

ii. Let us construct and consider a most elementary example of a multi-name credit derivative.

> First, we will collect 100 corporate reference debt obligations from 100 corporate entities, which are representative of a wide variety of industries (e.g., agriculture, manufacturing, real estate, etc.). Each name, or referent, has a notional value of $10 million: each referent is a generic financial asset; they collectively constitute 100 generic financial assets; they have a notional value of $10 million each. We pool these names together, which creates a portfolio whose total notional value is $1 billion.

Our reader is encouraged to remain mindful that here we concern ourselves only with *synthetic* replicas of 100 corporate reference obligations of $10 million

Table 2.1 Second, we then construct five sequential tranches of notional value, ascending in seniority, as follows

Tranche	*Notional Value*	*Attachment (%)*	*Detachment (%)*	*Leverage*
Tranche A	$840 million	16	100	1. 00
Tranche B	$40 million	12	16	6.25
Tranche C	$40 million	8	12	8.33
Tranche D	$40 million	4	8	12.50
Tranche E	$40 million	0	4	25.00
Total	$1 billion			

each; our portfolio has neither purchased nor invested in, and otherwise can claim no physical ownership of these 100 corporate bonds of $10 million each. If we *did* generically invest in and/or physically own such assets, and then proceeded to pool and tranche them, i.e., according to the methods of structured finance, we would now be elaborating for our reader the process of 'cash securitization,' or 'structured generic finance' – which is the process of securitizing generic financial assets. Here we are specifically concerned with 'synthetic securitization,' or 'structured synthetic finance,' which is a process for securitizing synthetic financial assets; and so all of our previous observations on single-name credit derivatives (in Notes 1–3) may be comported into our compounded understanding of structured synthetic finance herein.

From the example provided above, we see a concrete illustration of our earlier assertion – namely, that the *process of pooling* de-differentiates 100 increments of $10 million each worth of risks and cash flows into one portfolio of $1 billion worth of risk and cash flow; and then the subsequent *process of tranching* re-differentiates the now $1 billion worth of risk and its cash flow into 5 new classes of risks and cash flows – albeit the quantity and quality of these risks and their cash flows have materially metamorphosed, i.e., they have ontologically changed in kind. For this reason our reader will see why we say that structured finance is a technology for the fungible distribution of risk and cash flow. Moreover, we also see that we are synthetically 'repeating' the generic asset, but in the process of this repetition we produce a difference; we produce a new change in kind.

iii. Closer consideration of the nature of tranches will better illustrate this truth.

To observe that (a) the result of pooling 100 corporate names into a single portfolio is to homogenize their risks and cash flows into one asset with a single risk and single cash flow; and that (b) once we pool these names together, we can then re-differentiate this one risk and its cash flow differently and flexibly as we so choose – this is intriguing enough in itself.

However, our reader may have noticed an additional interesting material result of the process of structuring financial assets: by pooling 100 credit derivatives into a single synthetic financial asset, and then ontologically re-differentiating the risk and cash flow of this new asset through the method of tranching, a synthetically structured financial exchange involves the birth to actuality of several new economic properties which are specific to it, i.e., which were not originally 'in' or 'of' the generic financial asset acting as its referent. Anytime we use tranches to re-differentiate risk, there are 'levels of subordination' to the tranches, which have a series of 'attachment points' and 'detachment points'; this structuring process actualizes several new economic properties – for example, the properties of 'credit enhancement' and 'leverage' (among several others that we will not discuss herein). This is as unexpected as it is insightful, since it means that the synthetic asset begins by announcing itself as a mere replica of its generic referent, just as the synthetic exchange begins by appearing as an avatar of a generic financial exchange; but there is a new difference produced by its repetition, for there are new and novel economic properties brought into being which are not of the generic asset, and not present in the generic financial exchange whose asset acts as the referent to the synthetic exchange.

Let us briefly define and consider these properties.

Levels of subordination are defined as the order of seniority of risks and cash flows among the different tranches. An *attachment point* is the point at which losses attach to a particular tranche. And a *detachment point* is the point at which losses detach from a particular tranche, in order to attach to a different tranche with a higher level of subordination. The effect of tranching is the organic creation of such *points*. And the effect of these points is the organic creation of *credit enhancements*, which are various amounts of credit support provided to the different *levels of subordination*. This, in turn, amounts to the embedding of leverage into the exchange: it infuses the property of natural *leverage* into these levels (*leverage here being defined as the deployment of debt to augment the volume and speed of gains and losses*).

For instance, in the example provided above we have arranged Tranche E as the most *junior level of subordination*, with an *attachment point* of 0 percent, and a *detachment point* of 4 percent. Tranche E is therefore exposed to the risk of the total portfolio, insofar as the first dollar of any loss in notional value to the synthetic portfolio is absorbed by Tranche E, but materially affects none of the other Tranches. Correlatively, the first dollar of appreciation in notional value beyond the $1 billion valuation in the portfolio – which is to say any increase in profits beyond the amount agreed to at the commencement of the synthetic exchange – is enjoyed by Tranche E, but materially affects none of the other Tranches. For this reason we say that Tranche E is the 'equity tranche' in the synthetic portfolio, but that all of the other Tranches are 'debt tranches.' And of course all of the levels will have various amounts of expected yield, agreed to at the commencement of the transaction. So for example, Tranche E will obviously have the highest expected yield, given that E assumes the greatest amount of risk.

Because we know that Tranche E has a notional value worth $40 million in a portfolio whose total value is $1 billion, we see that the Tranches have been arranged such that Tranche E will continue to absorb all losses to the portfolio until such time that $40 million (or 4 percent) of the total notional value of the portfolio has been depleted – at which point the risk to the portfolio will detach from Tranche E, and then attach to Tranche D. Therefore, we can see that Tranche E provides a 4 percent level of *credit enhancement* to the other Tranches. But as we just noted, there also is no ceiling on the increased profits enjoyed by Tranche E, if and as the notional value of the total portfolio appreciates beyond $1 billion. This means that Tranche E, whose value is only $40 million, is exposed to the total returns and losses on a $1 billion portfolio – in other words, Tranche E is *leveraged* 25 times (i.e., $1 billion ÷ $40 million = 25). This is the meaning of our statement that Tranche E is the most junior level of subordination, with an attachment point of 0 percent, and a detachment point of

4 percent, provides 4 percent credit enhancement to the other Tranches, and has a leverage ratio of 25.

At the top end of the example provided above, we have arranged Tranche A as the most *senior level of subordination*, with an *attachment point* of 16 percent, and a *detachment point* of 100 percent. Tranche A is therefore not exposed to any risk of the $1 billion portfolio until the total notional values of Tranches E through B have been completely wiped out. For instance, once the first $40 million from Tranche E is wiped out, which is 4 percent of the total notional value of the portfolio, Tranche D begins absorbing subsequent losses in the portfolio up to 8 percent; at which point the losses to Tranche D detach, and Tranche C begins absorbing all subsequent losses up to 12 percent; at which point Tranche B now attaches, and begins to absorb all subsequent losses up to 16 percent of the total notional value of the portfolio of names.

Because we know that Tranche A has a notional value of $840 million of a portfolio whose total notional value is (or was, to begin with) $1 billion, up until the time that $160 million (or 16 percent) of the total notional value of the portfolio has been depleted, Tranche A remains materially unaffected by the losses to the other Tranches. Consequently, Tranche A is exposed to comparatively less risk than the four Tranches with lower levels of subordination, and has comparatively little, and in fact almost no leverage whatsoever. Tranche A also provides no credit enhancement to the other levels. As a result of all of these factors, the expected yield of Tranche A will be comparatively less than the other Tranches.

Note 5 Credit linked notes

i. The risk and cash flow attached to a Tranche is represented by the value of a credit linked note. Credit linked notes (CLNs) are an instrument for fusing multi-named credit derivatives with structured finance. They are therefore a means for redistributing risk and cash flow throughout capital markets by a process of structured synthetic finance.

A CLN is a debt note, or obligation, sold for a sum to an investor by an issuer, wherein that note represents a commitment by the issuer to make a principal payment due at maturity, or a coupon payment periodically, and whose value and yield is agreed to ahead of time – but whose value and yield is written down contingent to occurrence of a credit event (Figure 2.3). For this reason, the simplest way to begin to understand a CLN is to think of a fully funded credit derivative in which the protection seller *prepays* to the issuer the notional value of the swap ahead of time, and in return receives periodic (re)payments over the tenure of the swap; but if a credit event occurs, the principal owed to the protection seller by the protection buyer for providing event protection is written down.

In other words, when a synthetic financial exchange makes use of CLNs, the payment for an event which has not yet happened is paid in full at the commencement of the transaction by the CLN investor, who is the protection seller. And then a payment for that nonevent is periodically made, *or rather returned* to the protection seller over the tenure of the transaction by the issuer, who is the

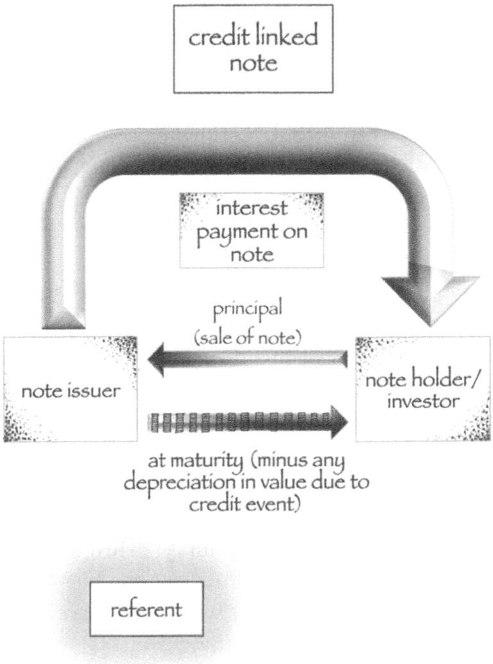

Figure 2.3 Credit linked note.

protection buyer – unless of course this nonevent eventually occurs. The terms of the exchange are backed by the issuance of a note, with a corresponding notional value: this note is a debt security, and as such, is a CLN.

ii. Let us consider an example of a CLN.

First, we pool and tranche 100 generic names of $10 million each into a synthetic portfolio of $1 billion.

Second, we wish to transform this unfunded multi-name credit derivative into a fully funded asset: to do this, the protection buyer will issue, or sell, CLNs to investors, with a total notional value of $1 billion. (Note: because this is a structured synthetic exchange, the CLNs are 'linked' to the notional value of different Tranches, and will therefore have various levels of subordination, credit enhancement, and leverage, and thus different amounts of risk, expected yields, cash flow, and possibly even different maturities.) By purchasing CLNs, the issuer prefunds the $1 billion synthetic portfolio.

Third, the CLNs yield a periodic coupon payment, whose amount is agreed to ahead of time; but they also carry a contingent payment feature. Over the tenure of the transaction, the issuer will continue to make coupon

> payments to the holder of the CLN, unless or until such time of occurrence of a credit event in the reference portfolio – at which point the notional value of the reference portfolio is written down, and in turn the coupon payments made to the holders of the CLNs are also written down. As the losses to the reference portfolio continue to accrue, so too is the interest on the notes and principal owed the holder of the CLN reduced.
>
> Lastly, at the termination of the transaction, the remaining principal is returned to the protection seller.

Let us consider the basic material significance of a CLN.

We earlier observed that a standard, single-name credit derivative is generally an unfunded asset, insofar as there is no invariance requirement on the collinearity risk and ownership. We also observed that this means, for instance, that the protection buyer – who is virtually detaching the risk and its cash flow from the referent in order to replicate and exchange that risk and its cash flow with the protection seller – need neither own nor have any other direct exposure to the generic asset whose event risk is replicated by the synthetic exchange. To any reader otherwise uninitiated in the peculiar materiality of credit derivatives, it is likely that this already looked rather topsy-turvy: 'How can one sell that or a part of that which they do not own?!' or, 'How can one buy event protection on an asset that they do not own?!' our reader will have marveled. 'Does the concrete principle of private property stand for nothing?!'

However, we should caution *this* reader that with the progressive differentiation of the CLN things have yet become more peculiar still. An unfunded credit derivative may have struck one as odd, or not; but its concept was always accompanied by the reassuring notion that the protection seller was being paid for a service of labor: namely, that she may or may not become the party responsible for repaying a generic debt obligation – contingent on occurrence of a credit event – to whose risk she was originally unexposed, but was now being paid *in advance* to assume. Conversely, the protection buyer was purchasing a guarantee on the risk of the reference asset, and so was naturally paying the protection seller *in advance* for assuming such risk. It was a synthetic exchange, inasmuch as no party to the synthetic exchange was party to the original generic financial exchange, whose asset provided the referent from which the synthetic asset was derived. But it was *enough like a classical exchange* of labor for wages, or rather wages *now* for possible future *labor*, insofar as the protection seller *may* have to provide a service of labor for the protection buyer in the future, and so is paid now for assuming this risk in the present. And it was *enough like a generic financial exchange of insurance*, insofar as the protection buyer was guaranteeing a level of value of the reference asset, and making a premium payment in the present, as an advanced charge by the protection seller for providing the guarantee of the level of value of the asset in the future. This portion of the transaction, at least, was surely partially acceptable to our uninitiated reader, even if they fundamentally regard credit derivatives as at base perverse, and otherwise desecrating the holy unity of property ownership and valorization of capital.

However, with the CLN we are now observing a method of *prefunding* a synthetically replicated exposure to risk and cash flow, and so have effectively reversed the temporal order of the distribution of cash flow among the parties, yet without reversing the spatial order of the distribution of risk. And for this reason, any ostensible similarities between either a classical exchange (of wages in advance for assuming the risk of service of labor in the future), or a generic financial exchange (of insuring the value of an asset in the future by making payment on its value in the present) now collapse. For now the CLN investor is buying from the CLN issuer a risk in a reference asset that the issuer does not own – but is also agreeing to pay in full and in advance for this risk. Correlatively, the CLN issuer is selling to the CLN investor a risk in a reference asset that the issuer does not own – but is being paid in advance for assuming the risk that *no* credit event in the reference asset will occur.

iii. There are several revelatory material effects that result from this method of synthetic exchange. We will only concern ourselves here with the most notable.

A CLN investor, as a protection seller, is purchasing from the CLN issuer the risk in the generic reference entity, just like the protection seller would do in any standard credit derivative transaction. Albeit now, by *prepaying* the issuer for this risk, the CLN investor has also purchased a generic risk in the issuer of the CLN as well. This writes another asset into the synthetic exchange that was not there from the start. Namely, this effectively creates an additional generic debt obligation, and therefore a new generic financial asset within the synthetic asset itself. For the CLN investor is now not only 'going long' the synthetically replicated reference obligation of the $1 billion portfolio, but has now also created a new generic financial asset through purchasing a risk exposure in the CLN issuer – which is to say that the CLN investor is now also 'going long' a generic financial obligation in the CLN issuer. In short, and importantly, this means that the CLN investor is synthetically invested in the material success of the reference entity, but therefore also generically invested in the material success of the CLN issuer. And this means that in reality the CLN investor is invested in both the material success of the $1 billion reference portfolio and CLN issuer alike. Unlike the unfunded single-name CDS, then – wherein the protection seller and protection buyer are involved in a zero-sum, high-stakes game, which one of the parties will 'win' and the other will 'lose'; now, by contrast, it is possible for both parties to benefit from the transaction – which means that synthetic exchange contains a non-zero-sum mode of economic transaction.

Relatedly, because the CLN is a device for converting a credit derivative as an unfunded asset into now a funded asset, we immediately become aware that there is a basic ontological difference between these two different synthetic incarnations – i.e., of an unfunded single-name credit derivative and a fully funded multi-name credit derivative.

We observed at the outset that single-name credit derivatives are unfunded replicas of funded generic financial assets, and so in this respect what defined the single-name synthetic asset – as an avatar of its generic referent – was precisely its unfunded nature. But now we see that the progressive differentiation of a

CLN signals the arrival of a mode of synthetic financial exchange that is, on the one hand, an exchange of a fully funded asset that is yet still synthetic, when what had previously distinguished the synthetic asset from the generic asset was precisely this basic ontological difference; but that on the other hand, it now turns out that this type of synthetic financial exchange is even capable of creating new generic financial assets ex nihilo.

That the synthetic asset is fully funded, and yet is nonetheless ontologically and a fortiori a completely different asset from any generic asset is observable by virtue of the fact that the synthetic asset has loosened many of the invariance requirements on the collinearities (e.g., on ownership, maturities, notional amount, and so on), and therefore has both more fungibility and a higher degree of symmetry than its generic counterpart. This, perhaps, at this stage in our investigations, is unsurprising, given its consistency with the ontological trend we have observed throughout our examination of synthetic finance. But to say the least, it is rather surprising to witness a method of generic financial exchange, and therefore a method for *the creation of generic financial assets* embedded within a technology for synthetic financial exchange. This tells us once again that you can derive the principles of generic finance from those of synthetic finance. And this also once more tells us that synthetic finance is a larger class of exchange than generic finance, since the former already contains the latter within itself, but not vice versa.

The question is what this means, ontologically and materially? This warrants a deeper look into structured synthetic finance. This is a future task for speculative materialism.

Note 6 Structured investment vehicles

i. In the beginning was the natural object. Classical exchange involves the conversion of a natural object into a commodity. Generic finance creates an asset from the commodity. And synthetic finance is the virtual replication of the generic asset – we have seen that in synthetic exchange we repeat the asset, but in the course of its repetition a new difference is produced. Structured synthetic finance, then, is the process by which a synthetic asset is transmuted into a security: the securitized asset has been divided, but in the course of its division it now changes in kind.

Securitization, whether cash or synthetic, involves the pooling (de-differentiating) and tranching (re-differentiation) of the risks and cash flow of the assets involved, and their subsequent redistribution in the form of the new securities that result. The vehicle used to accomplish this process is either a special purpose vehicle (SPV) or a structured investment vehicle (SIV).

Our ultimate concern here is with SIVs. However, because SPVs are the vehicular predecessors to SIVs, it is worth first observing their form and function in structured finance.

When financial assets are structured, any number of assets are pooled, packaged, and sold by their owner to an SPV: this vehicle is a shell of a company, or corporation, specially created by its originator for the purposes of structuring the assets, thereby recreating them anew as asset-backed securities, and issuing notes on these new securities to fund the operation. This means that the SPV purchases, pools, and tranches the assets, which in their new form (i.e., as securities) are 'backed' by their cash flow. Such asset-backed cash flows are sold as securities to investors, and are therefore called 'asset-backed securities' (ABS).[3]

Because the SPV, like all such vehicles, is a technology for creating securities from assets, it earns a fee for its labor; but to be clear, it is otherwise not a party to the structured financial exchange: the underlying assets from which the cash flows of the securities derive are *technically* owned by the investors – although this is already somewhat difficult to say, given that the materiality of the assets are no longer individuated assets, but have metamorphosed into securities, and all cash flows from the assets have now been divided into securitized cash flows, whose guarantee has taken the form of notes; and all cash flows 'pass through' the SPV on to the investors, according to the Tranche, its agreed-to terms of yield, level of subordination, etc. to which the notional value of their note is linked.

The SPV, then, acts as a master conduit, a vacuous assemblage, or rhizome through which cash *flows* – it is a hollowed substance, a kind of body without organs, whose role is to buy or replicate financial assets, turn such assets into securities, sell these securities to investors, and then pass this cash flow through itself and on to the originator. And then again, throughout the tenure of the structured financial transaction, it passes the cash flows from the ABS on through itself, but this time to the investors.

For this reason, we see and say that the SPV is a 'pass-through' vehicle. Moreover, it is bankruptcy remote, it has no legal right to any principal cash flow, and the whole of its life is limited to the transaction for which it has been exclusively brought into being: when its purpose has been accomplished, the SPV is not so much 'killed' or 'put down' as it now simply ceases to exist.

The historical development of structured finance involves the concomitant differentiation of SIVs from out of SPVs.

SIVs are just like SPVs in all aforementioned form and function, as outlined above. However, there is one dispositive ontological difference: rather than selling notes to investors that are directly tied to the cash flows from ABS, the SIV sells notes tied to the cash flow derived from the SIV itself.

In the case of an SPV, the structuring vehicle sells notes as a way of funding the purchase of assets and their subsequent transmutation into securities. This means that by buying the notes backed by the cash flows of the securities, investors are simulating property ownership of the assets, insofar as the SPV 'passes' the cash flow from the securitized assets 'through' itself and on to investors. However, the SIV sells notes to investors to fund its purchase and *holding* of the assets that it transmutes into securities. This means that investors are buying notes backed by the cash flow derived from the SIV, and the SIV is simulating property ownership of the assets, insofar as the SIV funds its notes payments to investors from the cash flowing to itself from the securitized assets – and so now the notional value of the notes is linked to itself, not to cash flow derived from the value of the securities. *This makes the SIV itself an asset-backed security.*

For this reason, we see and say that the SIV is a 'pay-through' vehicle. Moreover, this vehicle is not only bankruptcy remote, and not only has no legal right to any principal cash flow, but by virtue of its rhizomatic and non-substantive substance, it is a vehicle for the abolition of private property. Like the SPV, the whole of the life of the SIV is limited to the transaction for which it has been exclusively brought into being: when its purpose has been accomplished, the SIV is not so much 'killed' or 'put down' as it now simply ceases to exist.

ii. Let us reflect on the ontology of the SIV. There are three points to make, briefly.

First, we again observe a particular instance of relaxation on an invariance requirement, as part of the trend we have generally witnessed throughout our examination of the ontology of synthetic finance. In this case, we see that the *requirement on the collinearity of ratios of value* has been loosened.

In any instance of either a classical exchange or a generic financial exchange there is an absolute invariance on the collinearity of ratios of value. Whether it is a matter of buying and receiving $100 worth of a classical object, or buying and receiving the yield on $100 worth of a generic financial asset; in every instance the achievement of symmetry, and therefore the terms of the transaction, are predicated on a requirement that the notional value of the referent and the notional value of its cash flow should be absolute, invariant, i.e., that their ratios will not curve, bend, splinter, twist, or warp over the tenure of the exchange. There is an invariance requirement on the property of *the ratio of value* – and it is one that initially carries over into a structured financial exchange, but now over time, and especially with the transition from an SPV to the SIV, has been progressively loosened. How so?

We will notice that in an SPV-administered structured financial exchange, there is a total notional value to the reference portfolio, whose risks and cash flows have been securitized; and when the SPV sells the notes to investors, they also have a total notional value, whose risks and cash flows have been divided into Tranches – but at any rate, the terms of the exchange intend to align these two notional values, as if they were a pair of parallel lines, whose equidistant alignment will not curve or bend or twist or warp over the tenure of the exchange.

However, with a SIV-administered structured financial exchange, and in particular, with the transition from the structuring vehicle acting as a pass-through to now a pay-through vehicle, this invariance requirement on the ratios of value is loosened. Again, we see that there is a total notional value to the reference portfolio, whose risks and cash flows have been securitized; and again, when the SIV sells the notes to investors, they also have a total notional value, whose risks and cash flows have been divided into Tranches – but in this case, the terms of the exchange *do not align these two notional values, their ratios need not be arranged as parallel lines, their notional values may curve, bend, splinter, twist, or warp over the tenure of the exchange*. For this reason we will observe that the structured synthetic financial exchange which utilizes a SIV involves a loosened invariance requirement on the collinearity of ratios on notional values, and therefore has yet a higher degree of symmetry than the aforementioned like generic and synthetic versions of structured finance.[4]

Second, as we saw already in our consideration of CLNs (Note 5), we should not underestimate the profound material capacity of synthetic exchange to create new assets, with new and novel sets of economic properties – synthetically created, yes, but created anew nonetheless. The SIV shows us this once again. How so?

We know from our example, that the reference portfolio in the structured financial transaction is composed of credit derivatives, and is therefore ostensibly a synthetic replication of a generic financial exchange. Likewise, we have seen that the parties to the transaction are synthetic lenders and creditors, or sometimes both (see Note 7), depending on the arrangement of varieties of synthetic obligations, their spatiotemporal order of risks, and spatiotemporal order of payments. But now, with a SIV, we see that the CLN investor has also entered into a generic financial exchange with the vehicle itself – which is itself virtual and non-substantive, but for all that *no less a real entity*. This means that the credit linked note itself is both a synthetic and generic financial asset – but that also, quite unexpectedly, it is an asset whose status as a generic financial asset was only brought into being by virtue of first being a synthetic asset. In other words, in a structured financial transaction that uses SIVs to distribute CLNs, we are able to derive the generic asset from the synthetic exchange, rather than vice versa, and that therefore not only does a synthetic exchange exhibit a higher degree of symmetry, but it also now proves both a more original and more fungible way of creating financial assets – and ex nihilo at that.

Third, then, must be our Deleuzian question as we move forward – insofar as it is a question about the rhizomatic-character, the n-dimensional multiplicity of an SIV.

SIVs, like all such vehicles, (a) *have no past and no future*, insofar as they are convoked into being for the purposes of the transaction at hand, and when once completed are wound down; (b) *are discrete and limited*, in that they are prohibited from carrying on any other business not germane to the transaction; (c) *are nominal and independent orphans*, for their shares are public charity, they are bankruptcy remote, cannot be consolidated by any company or individual, and are not a subsidiary of their originator; and (d) *are therefore non-substantive shells*, i.e., a 'filling' of cash flow constantly passes through them, yet there is no essence of filling inside.

For this reason, in the future we will turn to Deleuze – for why he calls this kind of vehicle a body without organs, and shows that this is much more than simply a fun metaphor describing its ontological makeup. Indeed, we wish to know what, if any, is the historical-materialist meaning of this movement from a tree-like structure to the distribution of flows of finance capital, which has dominated the structure to intermediation for so long, but is now an increasingly rhizomatic, non-substantive, dynamical structure? This is a future question to be more thoroughly asked and addressed by speculative materialism.

Note 7 Synthetic CDOs

i. All threads of analysis from our previous Notes can now be woven into an understanding of peculiar material ontology of the economic object of a synthetic CDO.

Available literature on structured finance commonly defines 'cash CDOs' as structured generic investment products, whose securitized cash flow is sold to investors in the form of debt notes, and is backed by pools of assets culled from balance sheets, capital markets, or some combination of the two. Of course, we are, as always, ultimately only interested in synthetic finance, and therefore in synthetic CDOs herein. However, for this very reason our reader will permit us to make a brief observation about structured generic finance (also called 'cash securitization'), insofar as it will inform our historical-materialist understanding of the progressive differentiation of synthetic finance from out of generic finance, and in turn how these two classes of exchange – with their overlapping but different materialities, markets, and objects populating them – ontologically interrelate.

The concept and technology of the synthetic CDO has its historical origin in the cash CDO; and the concept and technology of the cash CDO has its historical origin in still earlier forms of structured finance – such as CMOs (collateralized mortgage obligations), CLOs (collateralized loan obligations), CBOs (collateralized bond obligations), and so on. However, what differentiates these other, prior, structured generic financial assets from the CDO in its particular structured generic financial guise is a basic difference in their compositions: while a CMO is solely composed of mortgages, a CLO solely of loans, a CBO solely of bonds, and so on, by contrast a CDO is an impure heterogeneous pool of varieties of assets, an adulterated mix of mortgages, bonds, loans, or any other kind of generic debt object, with different maturities, risks, and expected returns. In fact, the logic behind the CDO goes one step further than all previous forms of structured finance by reasoning that if it is simply a distribution of yields we are after, why not create a structured vehicle whose composition is a hybridized assemblage of generic and synthetic assets?

Therefore, the CDO is the first structured financial technology to consciously acknowledge that if it is the properties of risk and cash flow that constitute the valorization of finance capital, then any given number and classes of assets can be collected and hybridized, de-differentiated through the process of pooling, and re-differentiated anew through the process of tranching, thereby plastically changing their risks, cash flows, and other economic properties in kind, as well as thereby bringing new economic properties into being. For this same reason, today, to speak of 'synthetic CDOs' is increasingly anachronistic, since on the one hand this aforementioned discovery gives birth to the actuality of the synthetic CDO, and yet on the other hand over time we see that any earlier fixed, or observable ontological line of distinction between cash and synthetic CDOs is *regressively differentiating* into now a de-differentiated combination of both. In other words, the synthetic CDO signals the progressive differentiation of a class of exchange that does not preserve the previous ontological distinction between synthetic and generic assets – for in the process of securitizing different classes of assets, all differences become indistinct, indifferent, de-differentiated.

As speculative materialist political economists, we wish to know the material significance of this. Of what, if any, is the historical-materialist trajectory of this material development. Of what it means for the future of the dynamical system of economic transactions we call capitalism And how we should regard the relation of generic to synthetic finance when now a new class of exchange actualizes itself, and proceeds to regressively differentiate that which was previously differentiated, particularized, unitary, and distinct.

Quite obviously it is the case that generic finance *historically* precedes the material development of synthetic finance as a class of exchange, insofar as the latter has differentiated itself – linearly, historically, progressively – from out of the former. And yet we are constantly discovering and rediscovering in so many different ways throughout our study of credit derivatives that generic finance is *ontologically* a mere special case of that more general class of exchange that is synthetic finance. Indeed, if a synthetic CDO is a hybridized assemblage of generic and synthetic assets, while a cash CDO is solely composed of generic financial assets, this once again reveals that synthetic finance is an ontologically larger class of exchange then generic finance, for the former contains the latter within it, but not vice versa. This material development is illustrative of what can only be labeled as the *regressive differentiation of capital* in its synthetic-systemic incarnation. Our future speculative materialism must seek to draw out the deep ontological significance of this aforementioned if counterintuitive truth.

ii. Let us now consider an example of a synthetic CDO (Figure 2.4).

The first step is to de-differentiate a heterogeneous pool of risks and cash flows into a single, homogeneous portfolio. To do this, an originator will identify and select a pool of names, whose risks and cash flows are synthetically transferred into the portfolio. Let us say that the pool of assets comprising our portfolio has a notional value of $1billion.

The second step is to now re-differentiate this one risk and its cash flow into a set of new risks and new cash flows. To do this, we will create four Tranches (A, B, C, D). Each Tranche will have different risks, cash flows, levels of subordination, detachment and attachment points, credit enhancement, and leverage.

We must model a probability distribution for this pool of names. For example, our model may tell us that to get a D tranche, we need a credit enhancement of 2%. Let us posit that the most junior level of subordination will come from the originator. This means that the originator will be both a protection buyer on the portfolio of names, but is also initially invested in the material success of the portfolio: the originator will buy protection on the reference portfolio, but will also retain the first 2% loss to the notional value of the portfolio (for this reason, we will call this first 2% loss the 'threshold risk,' and the holder of this threshold risk – which in this case is the originator – 'the thresholder').

The third step is to create an SIV to execute the transaction. The order of its business will be:

(a) The SIV sells unfunded protection to the originator by way of CDS (although a TRS could just as easily be used) against the $1 billion reference portfolio, for a total value of $100 million over and above the first 2% loss, which is $20 million.
(b) The SIV sells $100 million worth of CLNs to various CLN investors. Because there are four Tranches, there will be four classes of notes, (A, B, C, D) corresponding to each Tranche (A, B, C, D), and each with a value of 2.5% of the $1 billion reference portfolio, which is $25 million per Tranche. Therefore, each class of CLN investor is both selling and prefunding event protection on the $1 billion reference portfolio.
(c) The combined material effect of a) and b) is that the originator has bought credit protection equal to the total notional value of the CLNs issued by the SIV.

The fourth step is for the SIV to use the cash raised by issuing the prefunded CLNs to invest in low risk, low-yielding securities, or some other ostensibly default-free collateral (e.g., government bonds are the common asset used; but they could be anything of this sort).

Let us consider the distribution of risks and cash flows to the parties involved in this synthetic financial exchange.

First, let us consider the SIV.

We will recall that, materially speaking, the SIV is an empty vehicle, a rhizome, whose sole purpose is the distribution of cash flows. But it is also *to begin with technically* the property owner of the synthetic assets – albeit the assets have metamorphosed into securities, and as such, have been divided up among the various CLN investors. This means that the SIV has been used to synthetically replicate property ownership among the CLN investors, yet without any ownership of property changing hands. Who owns the securities, and thus the risks and cash flows derived from the physical assets to which their value corresponds? The CLN investors do. The SIV has merely mediated the transaction.

The SIV receives cash flows from both the originator and the CLN investor alike: the originator is an *unfunded* protection buyer, who pays the agreed-to protection premium to the SIV. But the SIV in turn also buys *funded* protection from the CLN investors, receiving from them prefunded, up-front protection payments through a one-time sale of the notes, and from whose proceeds the SIV has used to invest in low-yielding, low risk securities, which are held as collateral. It is therefore meaningless to say that the SIV either stands to 'benefit' or 'lose' anything in the transaction, insofar as the SIV is a vacuous vehicle for the

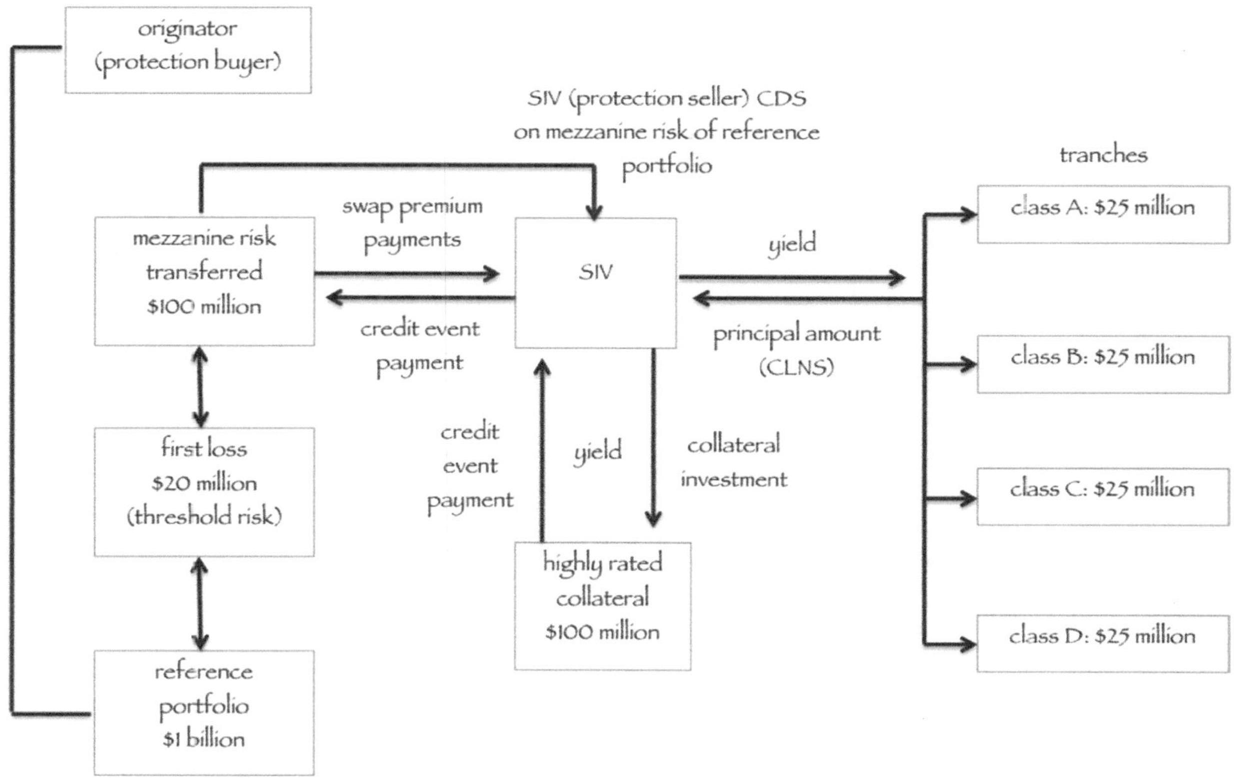

Figure 2.4 Synthetic CDO.

becoming of the distribution of risks and cash flows of the transaction, yet without ever fixing on a *being* of value for itself, per se.

Second, let us consider the originator.

The originator is a protection buyer, but also occupies the most junior level of subordination on the synthetic CDO. We defined a 2 percent detachment point as the portfolio's 'threshold risk' and the originator as 'the thresholder.' This means that the originator is providing 2 percent credit enhancement to all four Tranches, and as a result is the first party exposed to losses in the reference portfolio. In other words, a 2 percent natural leverage is embedded in the transaction by the originator's assumption of threshold risk.

However, anything over this first 2 percent loss to the portfolio (i.e., anything over the first $20 million loss) triggers a compensation claim by the originator to the SIV. If this happens, two things will now result: First there is a sale of the low risk collateral set aside by the SIV, and subsequent proceeds from the sale are made by the SIV to the originator; Second, and at the same time, the value of the CLNs are written down – with the ascending scope of losses first affecting Tranche D, then Tranche C, then Tranche B, and then Tranche A – until such time that the losses exceed 12% of the total notional value of the reference portfolio.

After the losses to the synthetic portfolio have exceeded 12 percent, the CLN holders are absolved of exposure to any future losses, and the originator is now left with a synthetically structured asset that is absent any risk or cash flow – and hence there is now no longer any value to the portfolio whatsoever.

Finally, this brings us to the CLN investors.

As we mention above, from 0 percent to 2 percent loss to the notional value of the reference portfolio, the premium payments made by the SIV to the CLN investors remain unaffected. However, once the 2 percent threshold has been crossed, losses to lowest level of subordination attach, which is Tranche D, followed by Tranche C, then Tranche B, and lastly Tranche A.

This means that from 2 percent to 12 percent loss to the notional value of the reference portfolio, or from $20 million to $120 million worth of losses, the CLN investors retroactively absorb the losses to the portfolio by writing down the value of their notes, and therein incur a cash flow reduction in premium payments made to them by the SIV. But because the CLN investors have prefunded their protection payments, once the Tranche to which their note corresponds has been detached from the transaction, all retroactive liability is terminated, and their role in the transaction is closed.

This means that the returns on CLNs have been leveraged by the Tranches above them (and even before that by each thresholder) by method of embedding levels of subordination into the exchange. However, it is worth observing that while this leverage is to begin with like any other kind of leverage – in that parties involved have actualized the right to a return on a base of capital whose principal exceeds the amount of their individual contribution – in other ways it is radically different from other kinds of (what we will call) 'artificial leverage,' in that the monetary downside of any losses is only an augmentation of risk in

reducing the value of their note to zero: they cannot, in other words, unlike in other kinds of artificially leveraged transactions, lose more than they have 1.
invested; they can, however, as with other kinds of artificially leveraged transactions, earn a right to a return that exceeds what they have invested. For this reason, we see and say that structured leverage is an ontologically different kind of leverage than unstructured leverage. And for this same reason, structured leverage is what we call 'natural leverage' – i.e., it is natural and organic to the composition of its structure, which has the effect of augmenting the *volume* of gains and *speed* of losses, rather than artificially employed to augment both the volume of gains and volume of losses, the latter of which may fall below zero.

Ending with a modest proposal

i. Let us close by briefly reflecting on the nature, both actual and potential, of the structured synthetic reference portfolio. This, in turn, will allow us to reflect on the inherent, radical, nomadic distributive capacities of synthetic finance, and on the wholesale powerful materiality of credit derivatives as a class of synthetic financial exchange.

In the example provided above, we followed common financial industry practice when we pooled and tranched a collection of risks and cash flows, which were synthetically replicated from $1 billion worth of corporate names. However, an interesting and not unimportant speculative materialist question to ask here is: *what else could comprise our reference portfolio, and what would be its material effect*?

ii. For example (Figure 2.5):

Let us imagine that every individual – regardless of their race, vocation, lineage, socio-economic class, or gender – were to be an originator of their own synthetic CDO. A first thought may regard this as counterintuitive. However, once we have realized how such a synthetic CDO would be composed, this is perhaps not such a bizarre notion.

How would this be accomplished?

(1) On the one hand, we would identify and collect a *universal* pool of all risks and their cash flows into a single portfolio through the method of synthetic replication. This portfolio would be a synthetic portfolio, and as such, would comprise the 'base matter' for every individual portfolio. Then, an elementary accounting formula would allow us to combine as the notional value of the total referents for each individual's portfolio a co-equal split between (a) total GDP (gross domestic product), or even GGP (gross global product), and (b) an individual's annual taxable income. Each and every individual would then hold their own individual synthetic portfolio, and with its own partially codependent total notional value, which is determined by combining (a) and (b) by a common divisor.

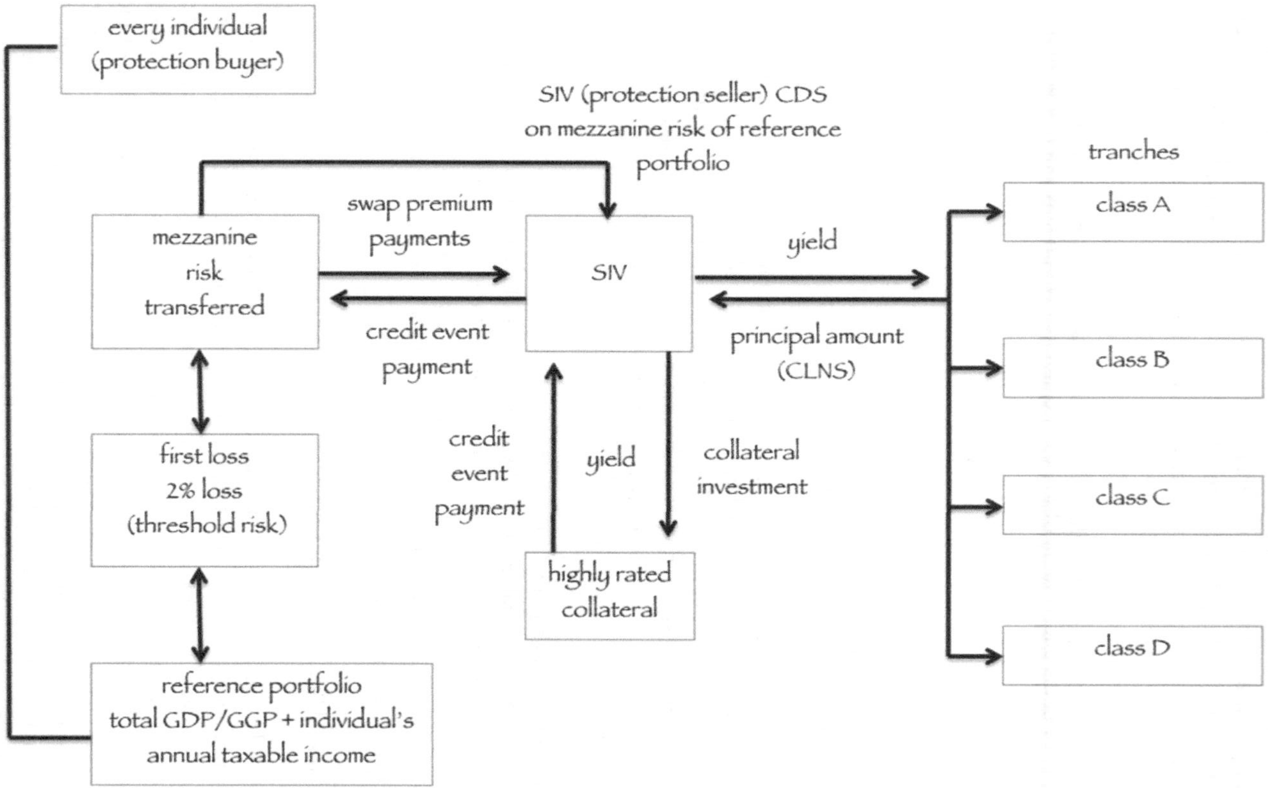

Figure 2.5 Universal synthetic CDO.

(2) If our reader at this time will please return to the example and Figure provided in 2.4, in order to compare the simple substitution of the following terms into Figure 2.5, she will see that:

(a) as the synthetic portfolio: 'total GGP+an individual's annual taxable income' is put in place of '$1 billion of corporate assets'; and
(b) as the originator: 'every individual' is put in place of 'XYZ protection buyer'; and now
(c) as the CLN investor/note holder: the various 'Tranches' will be occupied (in the form of note holders) in an ascending scale of 'every individual,' based on their annual taxable income – or really for that matter, on any other qualification we wish to agree on.

Our reader will now see that:

(3) This set of very simple acts will simultaneously tether each reference portfolio to a combination of collective and individual wealth, while tailoring each synthetic transaction to an individual's distributive needs. We have created a synthetic CDO, which uses the circulation of synthetically replicated risk and cash flow to universally distribute risk and cash flow when and if it is needed. There has been no appropriation of private property (at least not up-front and ostensibly), no authoritarian-induced shift in society's current mode of production or consumption, nor any centralized reallocation of wealth. No one – to begin with – has changed their vocation, their employment status, or anything else of the like.

And yet the wager of our speculative materialism is that by restructuring the mode of circulation, a new mode of structuring the interrelations of production, consumption, distribution, and circulation may actualize herein.

A final point, then, is that there is no physical or generic financial limit to the assets whose risk and cash flow we wish to synthetically replicate. Moreover, these thoughts – i.e., of what then can be done – only open up to us once we begin to grasp the fungible character of synthetic assets, the de-differentiating and re-differentiating capacities for different risks and cash flows that result from the process, technology, and class of exchange that is synthetic finance. Consequently, these are future topics to be examined by speculative materialism.

Notes

1 All material used for examples, figures and tables in Essay Two are reworkings of material culled from Vinod Kothari, *Credit Derivatives & Structured Credit Trading*, Wiley, 2009.

2 LIBOR (or London Interbank Offered Rate) is a globally used primary benchmark for interest rates.

3 ABS is the general term used to denote any variety of securitized generic financial assets, whether based on mortgages (MBSs), collateralized commercial loans (CLOs), collateralized corporate bonds (CBOs), collateralized insurance obligations (CIOs), and so on.

4 For more on measuring degrees of symmetry in exchange, please see the Appendices, 'Two Kinds of Symmetry, Three Classes of Exchange.'

3 Wagers of the synthetic

Difference & Repetition as heterodox political economy

Introduction

i. When meditating for a period of time on *Difference & Repetition* (*DR*), one is increasingly struck by an awareness, peculiar though it is, that while Deleuze composed *DR* as a book of philosophy, it is also very suitably read, perhaps most deliberately, as a work of heterodox political economy. In actuality *DR* is an abstract, pure, high-theoretical text, giving philosophical transformation to mathematical and scientific concepts, through its difficult and dense but ultimately rich exposition of the overlapping dynamical orders of difference and repetition: Deleuze, throughout, illustrates the deep ontology of difference and repetition, irreducible and universal to any dynamical system.[1] But then again when read as political economy, the book's final intention flips forward into the proposition of a radical alternative concept of value, predicated on the profound, historical-materialist, monstrous ontological power of the synthetic. And this itself is a possibility, if only because difference and repetition are also irreducible to the set of dynamical systems collectively called the economy, which progressively actualizes the system of exchange called finance.

Those readers of *DR* who have closely attended the progress from our inaugural attempt to think the material properties of synthetic finance in Essay One, to then our case study on synthetic finance in Essay Two, will no doubt already have begun to know why we now turn to a book whose vocation is an exposition of the relation between difference and repetition. These two concepts, for us, now denote the *difference* produced ex nihilo and ad infinitum from synthetic *repetitions* of generic financial assets. The synthetic is a replication, though not of the same; a production of pure difference in itself, yet always announces itself as simulation; the image of an object without likeness; an immanent copy of a model which quickly overturns any grounds on which such a distinction would stand.

ii. To this end, we saw the movement of our own analysis already yield two insights, which Deleuze's work will now help us to further expand: namely, of the (a) augmented symmetry, and (b) hyperfungibility of the synthetic.

Let us recall.

Synthetic symmetry

i. We know that there is a quantitative and qualitative increase in symmetry marking a synthetic exchange. Deleuze illustrates that this is a result of the difference produced by repetition.

We saw that the synthetic asset is yes, ostensibly replicated, or 'derived' from the generic referent. But also that its class of exchange loosens the invariance requirements on the economic properties of the object, and especially on the collinearities whose invariance is required by the other two referent classes of exchange, or what Deleuze will call 'flat space' classes of exchange. This progressive 'loosening' concomitant with the development of synthetic finance, as a result, gives birth to new and different economic properties, which were previously undifferentiated, immaterial, unactualized. For this reason we saw that synthetic finance is a larger class of exchange, since it contains generic finance and classical exchange within itself, but never vice versa. While it is the case that every exchange involves the repetition of an object into its image of value – which is to say that every exchange involves a transformation that achieves a symmetry between an object and its image of value as money – it is also the case that the class of exchange that is synthetic finance contains a higher degree of symmetry, but that this incremental change by degrees now amounts to and signals a qualitatively fundamental change in kind. In synthetic financial exchange the asset is repeated; and in the process of its repetition a new difference is produced therein.

For example, we observed the differentiation of the new properties of 'natural leverage' and 'credit enhancement,' among others, when considering the process of pooling and tranching endemic to structured synthetic financial exchange. And instructively, we observed that natural leverage is ontologically a wholly different kind of leverage than the 'artificial leverage' employed in any unstructured generic financial exchange. We saw that natural leverage is natural and organic to the composition of its structure, which has the effect of augmenting the volume of gains and speed of losses (but never the volume of losses below zero), rather than artificially employed to augment both the volume of gains and volume of losses – as was, always has been, and always will be the case with the leverage exogenously incorporated into and deployed in an artificially leveraged generic financial exchange. To this effect, we saw that a synthetic CDO whose portfolio was composed and universally distributed in the manner by which we spoke at the end of our case study (please see our 'Ending with a Modest Proposal,' immediately following Note 7), could technically assume an infinite amount of natural leverage, which would also proceed to eliminate the same condition through which synthetic exchange, since its origins, has always been a zero-sum game.

Our wager, then – which we close our analysis in Essay Three herein by elaborating – is that it follows that this simple technological supplement to the current organization of the distribution of risk and cash flow will restructure risk and cash flow *writ large*. And that everyone will assume a natural leverage lent by and born by everyone else. For this is one essence of our speculative materialism: an infinite natural leverage, grounded in the ex nihilo, ad infinitum, non-linear power of the synthetic.

ii. Now, this is to merely recall one of the many examples we observed throughout our case study in which the repetition by the synthetic asset of the generic asset produces a new difference in kind. Already in our opening essay we began to ruminate on the progressive differentiation of specific economic properties concomitant with the development of different classes of exchange. To be clear, we could have even only focused on the difference produced in the repetition of the generic financial asset from its physical corollary of the classical object. We could have recalled this as our example, had we been merely interested to examine the ontological differences between classical exchange and generic finance.

For example, we could have focused on a mortgage qua generic financial asset as the economic repetition of a house qua classical object, or any other generic financial asset as the repetition of a classical object. Anytime an invariance requirement is loosened in the process of repeating – say, for instance, as in the example of a generic financial exchange, in which we see a loosening of the invariance requirement on the economic property of tenure (which in generic finance is now no longer defined as and required to be immediate settlement) – we see that a new difference is produced, or rather is introduced into actuality; which is to say that a new extensive economic property differentiates from out of its earlier classical economic incarnation.

So when, as in the case of a generic financial exchange of a mortgage on a house, the tenure of the exchange is no longer required to be immediate settlement – again, as had been the case when the house was paid for 'in cash,' and immediately exchanged by manner of classical exchange – the new property of maturity differentiates itself from out of tenure (formerly defined *only* as immediate settlement), and tenure now ceases to exclusively denote immediate settlement; the new property of interest rate differentiates itself from yield (formerly defined *only* as a simple one-time return or cash flow), and yield now ceases to exclusively denote one-time return or cash flow; the new property of default risk differentiates itself from general counterparty risk, and counterparty risk now ceases to exclusively denote simple fraud and other moral hazards. And subsequently, as with any generic financial exchange, the volume of the image of value of the object is now free to fluctuate over the course of the exchange as well.

In the final analysis, then, any historical narrative of the progressive differentiation of the generic finance from out of classical exchange, just as is the case with the progressive differentiation of synthetic finance from out of generic finance, would serve to instruct us of the pure performative force of repetition as a sovereign engineer of difference – a difference engineer, whose supreme spirit of creative repetition knows no physical limit. Indeed, this is why Deleuze remarks, as if in particular thinking about the relation between the progressive differentiation of these classes of exchange and their production of difference, that '[r]epetition is the formless being of all differences, the formless power of the ground which carries every [economic] object to that extreme "form" in which its representation comes undone.'[2] This is the creative power of repetition *qua exchange* we sought to elaborate throughout Essays One and Two.

iii. However, we should not allow our subsequent delight to learn this truth to cause us to overlook that a basic ontological difference 'in kind' marks synthetic finance from the other two flat space classes of exchange. Everything about their fundamentally different ontological genera drives Deleuze's philosophical disquisition on the synthetic. And we, too, independently stumbled onto a clearing from which we witnessed this in our own case study, which we should not quickly forget.

Indeed, if traditional political-economic thought today still implicitly pivots its so-called 'material' analysis along the distinction between a model and its copy, an original and 'true' value versus its 'mere' replicated image, we should perhaps be unsurprised why. Deleuze observes that anywhere the study of a dynamical system judges a 'copy' in terms of a 'derived internal resemblance,' as does traditional political economy, we will also detect a morally conservative ontological prejudice that carries over into its implicitly arranged, violenced-hierarchy, in which the pure difference of the synthetic will only ever come in last place.

This is clearly at work in current popular declamations against credit derivatives. Always today, morally and economically below 'the identity' of the self-reflexive physical object of classical exchange, and again below its 'resemblance' as a good copy of its model by the asset of a generic financial exchange, stands the sophist, the bad copy, a suspect, monstrous false power – the simulacra of the synthetic – whose replicated materiality is always perceived to have only ever been comprehensible in terms of these supposedly 'more original,' morally superior economic objects of classical exchange and generic finance.

However, we must not overlook that in the course of development of any dynamical system there is a twilight of the icônes. This is now the case with our systems of exchange – the interconnected system of economies still called 'capitalism' by some. For in the course of the progressive differentiation of our system of finance, i.e., of finance capitalism, in the course of its seemingly infinite movement towards an ever-increasing degraded likeness of all economic objects, as they proliferate and incessantly create themselves anew; and as we continuously move from copy to ever-new replica of copy of objects, 'we reach a point at which everything changes nature, at which copies themselves flip over into simulacra and at which, finally, resemblance or spiritual imitation gives way to repetition.'[3] Such a point signals the opening production of a new difference in kind – a perceptible, if torpid and incremental quantitative change by degrees that suddenly produces a radical qualitative change in kind. This is the differentiation to actuality of synthetic symmetry; and it is qualitatively different from the classical symmetry at work in the other two flat space classes of exchange.

iv. In this respect, our case study has revealed not one, but two kinds of repetitions, whose qualitatively different ontological genera – it is our good fortune to acknowledge – Deleuze has also independently elaborated. There is, yes, the exchange, the moment of symmetry between any economic object and its image of value as money; this is a repetition of the same, a generality and equivalence: the object is repeated, and its repetition is an ostensibly identical image of itself achieved in and as the value-form. But there is also a second kind of repetition. As Deleuze says:

> [W]e must distinguish two kinds of repetition. In every case repetition is difference without a concept. But in one case, the difference is taken to be only external to the concept; it is a difference between objects represented by the same concept, falling into the indifference of space and time. In the other case, the difference is internal to the Idea; it unfolds as pure movement, creative of a dynamic space and time which correspond to the Idea. The first repetition is repetition of the Same, explained by the identity of the concept or representation; the second includes difference, and includes itself in the alterity of the Idea.[4]

We have seen that this first repetition carries over into and still characterizes the repetition of a generic financial exchange, in which the classical object (e.g., of the house) is repeated in the generic asset (e.g., of the mortgage). While in generic finance the image of value of the object is now free to grow or shrink over the course of the exchange (something that the classical object could never do), there is no true qualitative difference produced by its repetition. For the generic asset merely signals a quantitative change by degrees; it seeks to accurately 'model' the physical object; it strives to preserve its identity; it seeks to 'represent' its value as external to the concept, i.e., it is a representation of the same.

We will also observe that the classical objects and generic financial objects populating their respective markets, while no doubt their symmetry is different by degrees, nonetheless populate the same domain of action, which following Deleuze, we have labeled 'flat space': the structure to their spaces of exchange are fixed and flat, which is to say they are Euclidean, comprised of a revolving, zero-curvatured structure. Flat space economic objects will move to and fro in their course of exchange, i.e., from one party to the next; and yet their exchange consists of 'an empty form of difference, an invariable form of variation.'[5] In their course of exchange 'things' may change, but they always change in the name of the same.

If we are willing to concede that hitherto heterodox political economy has often assumed that the proper starting place is labor, and that labor-as-production is the structuring principle par excellence for the other terms in the series of terms constitutive of capital (production, consumption, exchange, distribution, circulation), we have arrived here at the key analytical distinction between this aforementioned heritage and the heterodox political economy inaugurated herein. For Deleuze is encouraging us to be wary of inadvertently admitting into our analysis a conservative, surreptitiously normative commitment to a flat space of repetition.

Deleuze moves to distinguish such flat space – wherein the motions of exchange always re-inscribe the economic object within an 'internally derived resemblance,' a self-consistent, reflexive identity of the object – from the curved space of synthetic repetition that swallows up or obliterates its reflexive identity:

> One [repetition] is revolving, the other evolving. One involves equality, commensurability and symmetry; the other is grounded in inequality, incommensurability, and dissymmetry. One is material, the other spiritual.... One is a 'bare' repetition, the other a covered repetition, which forms itself in covering itself, in masking and disguising itself. One concerns accuracy, the other has authenticity as its criterion.[6]

Moreover, according to Deleuze, the radical observation to make here is that this apparently 'derived' or 'secondary' synthetic repetition is ontologically, even materially, at the locus of the 'referent' or the 'first,' i.e., the 'generic' repetition. This immediately clarifies their ontological relation:

> The two repetitions are not independent. One is singular subject, the interiority and the heart of the other, the depths of the other. The other is only the external envelope, the abstract effect. The repetition of dissymmetry is hidden within symmetrical ensembles or effects.... [I]t is the masked, the disguised, or costumed which turns out to be the truth of the uncovered.

Our reader will know that we already observed this in our case study. We too have observed that when a synthetic CDO issues CLNs, a generic repetition is derived from a synthetic repetition (Note 5). Therein we realized that far from it being the case that the value of the synthetic asset is predicated on, or 'derivative' of the generic referent, we saw that in fact the opposite is true. Deleuze too observes this truth, and subsequently proceeds to provide a most exemplary ontological description of the peculiar materiality of the synthetic asset:

> Necessarily, since this repetition is not hidden by something else but forms itself by disguising itself; it does not pre-exist its own disguises and, in forming itself, constitutes the bare repetition within which it becomes enveloped.[7]

Of course, we have already seen in Essay Two that the synthetic financial asset is precisely that which does not preexist its own disguise. We must therefore both further examine the material significance of this second, apparently more ontologically fundamental repetition; and as well, we must at least pose the question of what, if any, is the historical-materialist significance that this more radical kind of repetition has now differentiated itself into actuality? For if it truly is the case that, as Deleuze says, the 'first' repetition, the generalized repetition of all exchange has its 'interiority ... [at] the heart of the other, the depths of the other' – i.e., synthetic exchange – what does it mean that the economic objects spun into the actual by the 'second' and 'bare' repetition of a synthetic financial exchange now have a quantitatively augmented symmetry that amounts to a qualitatively new kind of symmetry, a synthetic symmetry that now changes in kind?

Hyperfungibility

i. The qualitative increase in symmetry marking synthetic exchange – synthetic symmetry – either lends or reveals a hyperfungibility to the economic properties constitutive of the asset, as such: not simply their power to be plastically extracted and injected wherever and to whomever; not simply also their power to be created ex nihilo and ad infinitum – important as both of these are; but also their power to affect their profound materiality on the terms of *all* exchanges, either linearly or nonlinearly.

We first began to examine this progressive ontological trend in our opening essay. And then as a concrete example in our case study in Essay Two, we observed that already in the single-name CDS and TRS the risk and cash flow endemic to a corporate bond, for instance, or any other generic asset, can either be stripped from it and redistributed to the counterparty of the synthetic exchange; or may even be created anew – in the event that no party to the synthetic exchange was party to the generic exchange whose asset the synthetic exchange has referenced and repeated; and that, moreover, this process could retroactively, at present, or even *avant la lettre* change the terms of any other generic financial exchange. Are we willing to follow our conviction that it is more than simply ironic that with the development of credit derivatives, we are now capable of hedging any and all manner of economic risks that have yet to actualize themselves, when the baseline notion of social and political-economic justice has always been that this possibility should be made actual?

This power of economic repetition truly illustrates the progressive fungibility, which now increasingly amounts to a hyperfungibility, of synthetic financial exchange as a class of exchange. In this respect, the instructive pedagogical benefit of our first attempt, in Essay One, to materially analyze the synthetic asset helped us to expose and demystify what we labeled 'asset-fetishism.' We now better realize the meaning of what Fischer Black first observed in his 'Fundamentals of Liquidity' (please see 'Cash Flow' in Essay One): namely, that the identity of any economic object is dissolvable into a fragmentation of different economic properties – i.e., that properties, as differences, swallow up the apparent identity of the economic object (e.g., as this or that corporate bond, residential loan, fixed-rate mortgage, dividend-paying share of stock, and so on) into now a formless mess of partial objects that can be plastically stripped and injected elsewhere, or created or destroyed ex nihilo, ad infinitum, and nonlinearly. Moreover, as Deleuze observes, if new and different economic properties constantly 'swarm in the fracture' of the repetition of the object, i.e., are 'constantly emerging on its edges, ceaselessly coming and going, being composed in a thousand different manners,'[8] then to speak of any given economic object as having an 'essence' is a bit silly. For the essence of an economic object 'is nothing but an empty generality,' which means nothing apart from the object's many different economic properties.[9]

ii. For this same reason, Deleuze posits that 'the simulacrum is the true character or form – the "being" – of that which is.' Synthetic exchange signals the birth to actuality of a hyperfungible power capable of dissolving the identity of the asset; it is a return, or repetition of an asset that yet has no pre-constituted identity; it interiorizes the conditions of its own repetition as value; it is the value of repetition; *it is repetition as the interiority of value in itself.* As Deleuze observes:

> When the identity of things dissolves, being escapes to attain univocity, and begins to revolve around the different. That which is or returns has no prior constituted identity: things are reduced to the difference which fragments them, and to all the differences which are implicated in it and through which they pass. In this sense, the simulacrum and the symbol are one; in other words, the simulacrum is the sign in so far as the sign interiorizes the conditions of its own repetition. The simulacrum seizes on the *disparity* in the thing from which it strips the rank of model.[10]

How can we fail to recognize that Deleuze's depiction of the simulacrum isomorphically maps directly onto, and now further illuminates the profound meaning of our independent observation in our case study that the synthetic asset always begins by announcing itself as a copy (derivative) of a model (generic referent), but then proceeds to strip the latter of its rank as model? That it quickly 'swallows up or destroys every ground which would function as an instance responsible for the difference between an original and the derived, between things and their simulacra'? And that it, therefore, 'makes us party to a universal ungrounding' – where by 'ungrounding,' Deleuze intends to denote the 'freedom of the non-mediated ground'[11] of the synthetic, a repetition 'by which the very idea of a model or privileged position is challenged or overturned.'[12]

Finally, then, if we are no longer content to regard the asset qua economic object as having an inherent or fixed essence, but rather now conceive it as a moving horizon of fungible economic properties – any of which are capable of being stripped and re-injected elsewhere, but which can also warp, fold over, bend and twist – Deleuze reassures us that we are still able to 'think' the asset, as such. Albeit we are now thinking the asset as a multiplicity. And if this is the case, the question is then what kind of multiplicity is it?

Speculative materialist communism

i. From this vantage point, and at this stage in our analysis, our reader will have begun to understand what we mean when we assert that 'difference' and 'repetition' are the principal concepts of a book by that same name, *written* by Deleuze as a book of philosophy, but which can be *read* as a book of speculative materialist political economy, wherein the beginnings of a radical alternative concept of value, of ordinal value, is proposed. Moreover, in the opening lines of *DR* Deleuze distinguishes his heterodox approach from any hitherto conservative, Euclidean, *sedentarist political economy*, by noting that his concept of value is founded *not* on 'the qualitative order of resemblance and quantitative order of equivalence.' But rather, it is a concept of value founded on difference and repetition, organized around a mode of circulation endemic to synthetic symmetry.

Deleuze is therefore proposing not simply a concept of value, but a theory of a concept of value that effects a dynamical system of institutions, which in turn are capable of achieving a nomadic distribution of economic space. In other words, he is proposing *a kind of communism, albeit it is a communism of speculative materialism*. One way of stating the wager of Deleuze's political-economic project, then, which we now wish to adapt as our own, is the following:

> [W]hen we discover the literal interior meaning of [synthetic] repetition, we have the means not only to understand the outer repetition as a cover, but also to recapture the order of generality (and ... to carry out the reconciliation of the singular with the general).[13]

This is a seductive wager indeed. That the historical-materialist impetus of synthetic finance should actualize both a technology for the hyperfungible distribution of risk and cash flow, and relatedly, the inaugural abolition of private property (which is not the same thing as personal property), but also at the very same moment that structured finance opens its portal to universality, is our cause of justification for attaching the label 'a communism of speculative materialism' – a *speculative materialist communism*: in Deleuze's words, a 'discovery' of the 'literal meaning of repetition,' whose 'understanding' allows for the 'recapture' of 'the order of generality' – a means through which, finally, we might 'carry out the reconciliation of the singular [viz. the particular, the individual] with the general [viz. the universal, the global].'

ii. However, here our fellow passengers may wonder, is not the historico-economic baggage accompanying the term 'communism' far too weighty to accompany the 'speculative' on our flight?

> 'One personal item and one carry-on, only, please' – our flight attendant politely informs the passengers, as they proceed to board their flight ...

Our flight attendant is perfectly aware of the popular, if only partially conscious expectation that, given the poor forced choice of one over the other – i.e., either our personal item or a carry-on – we may be sorry to have to choose; but because we have always been led to believe that our (singular) personal item is the 'speculative,' and our (general) carry-on is 'communism,' when faced with the choice of one or the other, we will always choose the former. (After all, why else do we stuff our *truly* essential articles into our personal item, if not with the thought we always still risk having to 'check,' i.e., leave behind, our carry-on at the gate immediately prior to boarding, in the event that there's simply 'not enough space' on the flight?)

The trick for Deleuze, however, is to realize that in an era that bears witness to the reign of the synthetic, the speculative is no longer our singular personal item, but is now our general carry-on! This means that, correlatively, our personal item *is* communism. For this reason the wager of speculative materialism is that today, for the first time in history, what is equitable is now most profitable as well – that today individual profitability increasingly *demands* the equitable; and this precise point is what our material institutions continually scream out to us amidst incessant market crises; that such crises are themselves a result of mistaking the speculative for the personal, of treating the synthetic-speculative as a personal activity, when its technology is actually fitted for the general.

And because this means that the general *is* the speculative, we must be prepared to accept a communism that still goes by that name, but now denotes something quite different from its traditional historical-materialist expectation. For this reason, we have first sought to observe that multi-name credit derivatives are a technology for the administration of the abolition of private property, and structured synthetic CDOs are a technology for universalizing the equitable (which is not the same as equal) distribution of risk and cash flow.

Our new travelers' baggage for this leg of our journey, therefore, in other words, is not your grandfather's luggage, e.g., it contains neither a leather cap nor a tobacco pipe. In fact, what Deleuze so profoundly illustrates throughout *DR* is that the shared ideology threading its way through all prior leather-cap communism, as well as tobacco-pipe socialism, but also those unapologetic proponents of bubble-gum capitalism, is their implicitly held sedentarist conception of distribution. But we have seen that this presumption is a byproduct of a bad ontology. And because the shared sedentarist ideology threading its way through this three-in-one position has pre-structured the fixed, binary, Euclidean terms of their ensuing debates, a rejection of this bad ontology is precisely what distinguishes any other political-economic ideology whatsoever and our speculative materialist communism. For the radical terms of our wager is that the monstrous power of the synthetic – when wedded to the fidelity of a reconciliation between the general and the singular – is capable of effecting a nomadic distribution of economic space.

We formulated the *first ontological principle of our speculative materialism* at the end of the opening essay. We then made our *modest speculative materialist proposal* at the end of our case study. It only remains for us to now elaborate what the distribution of nomadic space entails, how such distribution is made available by the synthetic, and the concept of value that will aid us in operating the institutionalization of such a speculative materialism.

Nomadic distribution

i. Let us defer to Deleuze's phraseology of the issue between sedentary and nomadic distribution. But in truth, we must alert our reader that what is at stake herein is also a distinction between two kinds of multiplicities: numerical multiplicities, those zero-curvatured multiplicities of fixed, metrical, Euclidean space; and qualitative multiplicities, the curved multiplicities of n-dimensions, topological, and non-Euclidean. For this reason, we will follow our discussion of nomadic distribution – which involves a distribution of the (virtual) structure to the space of the actual – with a discussion of the register of the virtual, and then of qualitative multiplicities in more depth.

First, on sedentary distribution:

> We must first of all distinguish a type distribution which implies a dividing up of that which is distributed: it is a matter of dividing up the distributed, as such.... A distribution of this type proceeds by fixed and proportional determinations which may be assimilated to [numerical, metrical] 'properties' or limited [i.e., contained, absolute, fixed, Euclidean] territories within representation.[14]

But there is a second kind of distribution, the difference in repetition whose power resides with, or is grounded by, a synthetic symmetry.

This is nomadic distribution:

> [T]here is a completely other distribution which must be called nomadic ... [which is] without property, enclosure or measure. Here, there is no longer a division of that which is distributed, but rather a division among those who distribute themselves in an open [or (what Riemann labeled) an 'unbounded'] space – a space which is unlimited, or at least without precise limits.[15]

How can we fail to recognize that this nomadic distribution is, first, precisely the kind of distribution made possible by the peculiar materialism whose ontology we began to examine in our opening essay, and labeled therein as our first ontological principle? And that, second, this type of distribution is that which is actualized by a universal synthetic CDO (i.e., whose reference portfolio is universally composed and universally distributed), as we modestly proposed at the close of our case study?

ii. Deleuze further itemizes the differences between a sedentary and nomadic distribution.

On the order of nomadic distribution, there are several features of which we should take note.

(a) On the one hand: 'Nothing pertains or belongs to any person, but all persons are arrayed here and there in such a manner as to cover the largest possible space. Even when it concerns the serious business of life, it is more like a space of play, by contrast with a sedentary space and nomos.'

(a.1.) Deleuze is asserting that nomadic distribution involves a certain universality – albeit it is a universality availed of our traditional conception of distribution, which has thus far always been predicated on a bounded, sedentary, metrical, 'filling-up' of flat economic space. When the sedentary political economists – again, whether communist, socialist, or any variant of capitalist – argue over who gets what, where, and how, their shared belief is a presumption about a distribution of cash flow 'in' space, a distribution of objects in a pre-produced space, wherein all such subsequent distribution necessarily involves a 'filling-up' of flat, ambient, Euclidean space. Under this conception of distribution, space is a container of essentialized economic objects. Those objects have value. Their value is finite. Their finite value is exchanged for the images of objects as money. And money, as the image of value of the object, *represents* the object by obliterating all qualitative differences in the name of the identity of the same, i.e., in and as the commodity-form.

(b) But Deleuze clarifies here that, on the other hand: 'To fill a space, to be distributed within it, is very different from distributing the space.'

(b.1.) This further clarifies an irreducible difference between any leather-cap communism and our speculative materialist communism. Indeed, Deleuze is most definitely *not* speaking of 'a type of distribution which implies a dividing up of that which is distributed'; he is certainly *not* denoting 'a dividing up of the distributed, as such.'[16] All hitherto political-economic ideologies have thought about, proposed, debated, and politicked over distribution in precisely such aforementioned sedentary terms; but this is precisely what Deleuze is urging us to reject.

For this reason, whenever we hear that we need to *re-distribute* that which is, was, or will be *produced* in a certain manner, we immediately know that this argument can only proceed as it does because the activity of distribution is preconceived as a zero-sum game, insofar as what is distributed is a secondary, less original, temporally subsequent activity to production: distribution is conceived to be limited, metrical, and finite, i.e., the sedentary distribution of either scarce or plentiful resources – but which are at any rate finite.

(c) However, the wager of speculative materialist communism is that synthetic finance provides a new mode of distributing economic space itself – that this kind of distribution *is* a production of economic space, which has profound causal effects on our mode of production, as such; and that therefore synthetic finance provides us with a lock-and-key mechanism for reconciling the singular and general, yet which is *not* predicated on a *re*-distribution of risk and cash flow in pre-distributed economic space, but rather a distribution of risk and cash flow as the production of economic space itself.

We may need to model this wager. If this is modeled by our game theorists and quantitative analysts, but then again designed by and implemented by 'us,' i.e., a universal 'we,' this will amount to the inauguration of a radical political-economic project, a project for radically restructuring our economy, a political economy structuring the radical difference in repetition as its concept of value.

(c.1.) Lastly, then, if synthetic finance is in fact capable of carrying such a heavy load, if synthetic finance truly is that monstrous vehicle capable of bearing the combined weight of all the world's carry-ons and personal items as we commence on this leg of our journey; but also if, in turn, all sedentary political economists have hitherto fixated on the evils of synthetic finance, Deleuze reminds us once again that we should not be surprised:

> Such distribution is [always regarded as] demonic rather than divine, since it is the peculiarity of the demons to operate in the intervals between the gods' fields of action, as it is to leap over the barriers or the enclosures, thereby confounding the boundaries between properties.... The leap here bears witness to the unsettling difficulties that nomadic distributions introduce into the sedentary structures of representation.[17]

iii. Let us take heart, then, as we proceed. It was for this very reason we inaugurated our case study on synthetic finance in Essay Two by imploring our reader to indulge the prospect that in the course of our encounter with credit derivatives and other synthetic financial objects, it may turn out that their progressive differentiation from generic finance signals an important phase transition in our dynamical system of economic institutions, with deep historical-materialist significance. Was this not, from the outset of our case study, an appeal to our reader to be wary of allowing a crude moralism to creep into our study of the materiality of the synthetic?

As is fitting, we will defer to Deleuze here by closing with an observation that just as '[t]o rescue difference from its maledictory state seems, therefore, to be a project for the philosophy of difference,'[18] so too does our speculative materialism seek to rescue political economy from its current maledictory state, whereby the latter is conceptually incapable and aesthetically unwilling to proceed with a project of politically, economically, and even mathematically and scientifically thinking the monstrous power of synthetic capital. Speculative materialism is the method, set of wagers, and project which seeks to break this deadlock.

Virtual objects

i. Today, we commonly hear that synthetic financial assets are (colloquially) virtual. Let us allow Deleuze to probe this allegation.

In the course of *DR*'s exposition of synthetic repetition, we eventually discover that Deleuze is elaborating the register of the virtual. Of course our task here must include an exposition of this register of reality – to understand that while virtuality is neither actual nor potential, it is nonetheless a register of reality (Deleuze speaks of a reality of the virtual, *not* a virtual reality).[19]

Virtuality-Potentiality-Actuality: these are the three registers of reality. However, if we call the synthetic asset 'virtual,' is this not to propose to access the virtual? And is it not problematic to propose to access a reality whose supposed ontological status is by definition *not actual* – especially when the synthetic asset, if it is a so-called 'virtual object,' implies to us that it is also actual? For example, the synthetic asset is often colloquially deprecated on behalf of its alleged virtuality. But it is nonetheless convoked into being, it is metricized, its price series is modeled, it is exchanged, re-exchanged, and has concrete consequences. If the synthetic is virtual, is the virtual not also signified, a sign, an actuality?

There is an answer to this question. Let us begin to address it by concerning ourselves with Deleuze's exposition of the peculiar material status of the virtual object.

ii. Deleuze, to begin, provides the textbook definition of a synthetic object by more or less providing a textbook definition of a financial derivative, i.e., the derivative is an asset whose value is derived from an underlying referent. But he then observes, as we have, that things are not always as clear and simple as this.

We know, for instance, that many financial derivatives – and not only credit derivatives – can causally supervene on the value of a generic asset. In our case study we saw that credit derivatives can nonlinearly affect the terms of a generic financial exchange (Notes 1–3); or even that a generic asset can be 'derived' or 'deducted' from a synthetic asset. For example, when multi-name credit derivatives are used to compose a synthetic portfolio, and CLNs are issued to fund it (Notes 5–6), we saw that the value of the generic asset of the CLN is derived from the value of the synthetic portfolio.

For this reason we know that not only is the material performativity of the generic on the synthetic *not* a one way relation, but that vice versa is not exclusively true either, insofar as each is constantly and exogenously feeding into each other's interiority. We know that the synthetic asset is not only deducted from a generic referent, but in so many compelling ways is also incorporated in the generic referent. This is why Deleuze begins his exposition of the relation between the virtual and actual by observing:

> [B]y virtue of their dissimilarity and their difference in kind they borrow from and feed into one another. We see both that the virtuals are deducted from the series of reals and that they are incorporated in the series of reals.[20]

The challenge, according to Deleuze, is to understand that the virtual object is 'doubly inscribed' in reality – both as a partial object 'deducted' or 'derived' from a preexisting generic object in order to become actual, and in the process of this becoming, moves from the virtual into the actual; but more fully or comprehensively, it is also 'incorporated' into the whole of reality (including the virtual) therein. This is because the process from the virtual to the actual always points beyond itself, beyond the virtual, and towards the global integration of whole, identical, self-reflexive objects; while at the same time, the previously non-actualized virtual also continues to develop beyond itself, and as it does, moves into partial and non-totalized objects, a kind of relic of the virtual now uncomfortably housed in the actual and the virtual, simultaneously as one.

We will ultimately see that it is precisely this peculiar, hybridized, ontological status of the now partially actual virtual object that lends the synthetic its latent, monstrous, material supremacy.

But Deleuze first wants us to be clear that any profound ontological impact of the materiality of the synthetic object, whose repetition is the activity of the derivation, proceeds from this derivation itself:

> This derivation implies, first, an isolation or suspension which freezes the real in order to extract a pose, an aspect, or part.

This fact is as uncontentious and obvious as it is unilluminating for the student of credit derivatives. Of course it is the case that to 'extract' a currency risk, we simply write a currency swap; to 'isolate' an interest rate risk, we write an interest rate swap; if it is a matter of 'freezing' the risk of a credit event, we need merely write a credit default swap; and if one wishes to 'suspend' the totality of generic risks, then a total return swap is in order, and so on. Of course it is the case that a credit derivative 'extracts' an economic property from its referent. This *is* the basic essence of the technology and process of a swap that Fischer Black observed back in 1970, and with which we concerned ourselves in Essay One (please see 'Cash Flow').

However, Deleuze adds – as if encouraging us not to underthink what such a 'cleaved' or 'partial' status means for the ontology of this object:

> This isolation, however, is qualitative: it does not consist simply in subtracting a part of the real object, since the subtracted part acquires a new nature in functioning as a virtual object. The virtual object is a *partial* object – not simply because it lacks a part which remains in the real, but in itself and for itself because it is cleaved or doubled into two virtual parts, one of which is always missing from the other. In short, the virtual is never subject to the global character which affects real objects. It is – not only by its origin but by its own nature – a fragment, a shred, a remainder. It lacks its own identity.[21]

Let us consider the meaning of this assertion – that the virtual object is in reality 'cleaved or doubled into two virtual parts.'

It is interesting – but *not* coincidental – to see Deleuze invoke *actual* examples of virtual objects from discursive registers that are ostensibly utterly foreign to finance. For instance, Deleuze draws on psychoanalytic work done on the derivation of virtual objects, which both lack their own identity precisely because of their derivative status, but which also in turn quickly proceed to take on a life of their own, feedback into the valuation of the actual object from which they are derived, and effect a profound material performativity therein. Psychoanalysis shows us, for instance, Deleuze notes, that:

> The good and bad mother … [or] the serious and playful father … are not two partial objects but the same object in so far as it has lost its identity in the double.

Of course, he then adds,

> partial or virtual objects are encountered under various names.

In this respect – and whatever its discursive register happens to be – the virtual object acts as a kind of absent center around which the series of actualized objects circulate – yet without ever fully assuming or representing its vacant content. And the reason for this is that virtual objects and actual objects, while mutually and materially feeding into each other's interiority, do not resemble one another; they are ontologically different in kind:

> Although it is deducted from the present real object, the virtual object differs from it in kind: not only does it lack something in relation to the [actual] object from which it is subtracted, it lacks something in itself, since it is always half of itself, the other half being different as well as absent.[22]

The wary reader of *DR* who is uninitiated in the dark-theoretics of psychoanalysis may perhaps experience some puzzlement as to how this can be the case? Luckily for us, as students of synthetic finance, we experience no new puzzlement here: that the synthetic asset assumes the partialized status of a virtual object, and acquires a 'new nature' by virtue of its 'subtraction' from the actualized generic asset; and in turn, that such a synthetic asset is not subject to the requirements (or what Deleuze calls the 'global character') 'affecting' actual, whole, generic financial objects, is precisely what, throughout our prior examinations of credit derivatives, we have observed as the peculiar materiality of synthetic financial assets. It is no coincidence that we are able to draw on finance to cull examples to better illustrate Deleuze's work, for Deleuze is itemizing the ontology of the synthetic – and we are ontologizing its itemization as synthetic asset.

Deleuze identifies a number of rather unconventional characteristics marking the virtual object. What are they?

For one, we immediately see that the virtual object is ontologically unique from either potential or actualized objects in that it interiorizes difference in itself; and insofar as it does, its difference is capable of being thought, yet without being limited by the invariance requirements placed on identity, i.e., without ultimately being subjected to the requirements of classical representation. None of the self-reflexive, representational requirements of identity that supervene on flat space economic objects, whether classical or generic, are placed on the virtual object: it can bend over or twist, fold into itself or warp, double, divide, reverse, suddenly vanish and then reappear.

In this respect it is important to observe here just how far removed, ontologically speaking, the synthetic asset is from either classical or generic financial assets. The traditional and hitherto-recognized process of commoditization, or becoming-economic of the natural object, always-already implies a domain of action that is a flat space of exchange: a domain wherein the process of commoditization signals the operation of the value-form overcoming all differences, of subjecting individuated differences in the object to the self-reflexive identity of its value.

Marx, for instance, in the opening chapters of Volume I of *Capital* perspicaciously relays to us the itemized steps by which 'the different' is subject to a conversion of 'the same.' In a word, this is the process of rendering different quantities of qualitatively distinct objects commensurable, equivalent, and symmetrical. And we know this, still today, to involve the necessary metaphysical conversion of the natural object into the economic object. We know that this comes about from the 'grotesque' (in Marx's words) miracle of the value-form, as it collapses all differences (e.g., in Marx's examples: between cloth and coats, bibles and coffee, etc.) into the classical symmetry of value – and in the process, proposes to mediate or represent all differences, but only on condition of the object's radical preservation of its identity; and that this mediation is namely, the first principle of classical symmetry: the principle of reflexivity, i.e., A = A. If the object does not remain invariable in the course of its exchange, i.e., if A does not equal A when A is repeated, if the object does not equal itself when it is transformed into its image of value, the representation of the object's value will collapse, its symmetry will dissipate, and consequently, no exchange will occur. This is the original invariance requirement of classical symmetry at work in the value-form. It signals the obliteration of interiorized difference in the holy name of the same. It is both a necessary condition and result of the activity of commoditization concomitant with flat space classes of exchange.

However, the virtual object, as Deleuze describes it, is precisely that which suffers a radical destruction of its own pre-represented, pre-actualized identity in the course of its commoditization. In fact, this is precisely what synthetic repetition involves. Consequently, the partiality of its very identity, far from representing some kind of crude material shortcoming, is a crucial material feature of the synthetic asset, as such. If the classical representation of value requires both a global character to the object, and as well, demands that the economic object is reflexive and invariant in the course of its exchange, this is no longer the case with the virtual object.

This, then, reveals to us yet another peculiar ontological feature of the virtual object. Namely, it is not subject to the totalizing requirements of a fully actualized object.

Incidentally, this also helps us to account for why the synthetic asset is so open to the paradoxes of being. We have seen that in the course of its repetition, the synthetic asset both becomes what it is *and* what it is not: as an asset, it *is* what it is, i.e., it is a replicated incarnation of a generic asset; but it is also simultaneously *more* than what it is, i.e., it is both more fungible and has more symmetry than the generic asset, it can affect the terms of the generic exchange, it even acquires different economic properties than its generic referent; and yet it is also *less* than what it is, i.e., it is only a 'fragment' or 'shred' of its generic referent (for example, a currency swap replicates the currency risk but not the credit event risk of the referent, a credit default swap replicates the credit event risk but not the currency risk of the referent, and so on). In short, there is no one-to-one-mapping of the whole panoply of economic properties of the generic asset in the course of its synthetic repetition. Rather, it is merely a fragment or shred, a remainder. This is why Deleuze says that actual objects 'are subjected to the law of being or not being somewhere, by virtue of the reality principle; whereas virtual objects, by contrast, have the property of being and not being wherever they are, wherever they go.'[23]

However, Deleuze now also adds – as if encouraging us not to overthink what such a 'cleaved' or 'partial' status means for the ontology of this object:

> These partial or virtual objects are encountered under various names ... [but] these virtual objects are incorporated in real objects.[24]
>
> The virtual is opposed not to the real but to the actual. The virtual is fully real insofar as it is virtual...Indeed, the virtual must be defined as strictly part of the real object – as though the object had one part of itself in the virtual into which it plunged as though into an objective dimension.[25]

This, then, is the deep meaning of Deleuze's assertion that the virtual object is in reality 'cleaved or doubled into two virtual parts.'

Let us not misunderstand the ontology of the virtual object: it is not a matter of whether the virtual object can be either *only* virtual – and thus, as such, is immune to any representation in actuality – or whether it is a contradiction to say that the virtual is both actual *and* virtual. Rather, it is a matter of whether, and if so, to what degree the synthetic asset or any economic object for that matter is both a virtual object *and* an actual object – insofar as the virtual object is partially incorporated in all objects? In this respect, it is foolish to say that the virtual is *not* real. The synthetic asset, of course, *is* a real object. However, the interesting question arises when, on the one hand, we observe that the synthetic asset is indeed a partial object, a fragment, a shred, a remainder whose actuality has been 'derived' from another pre-actualized, generic financial object; but on the other hand, as we also observed in the course of our examination of the synthetic asset, the synthetic is incorporated, materially, in the generic asset, and is capable of changing it in kind. For again, as Deleuze emphasizes:

> Although it is deducted from the present [i.e., actual, generic] object, the virtual object differs from it in kind: not only does it lack something in itself, since it is always half of itself, the other half being different as well as absent. This absence, as we shall see, is the opposite of negative.[26]

Indeed, 'we shall see' that if the 'lack' or 'absence' of the virtual object is 'the opposite of negative,' it is because its partiality imparts to it the peculiar material status of being both a partially determined actuality, and yet also a partially undetermined structure without content. And it is this ontological feature of the virtual object that makes it an affirmation of difference in itself. Deleuze's point is that far from the lack in the virtual signaling a kind negation of being, rather it signals a pure affirmation of the conditions for all actuality – it is pure difference without concept; a pre-represented difference, capable of being thought, yet has not been fully differentiated in actuality. The morphogenesis of any economic object, its cash flow and risk, its materiality and value, occurs 'between the virtual and its actualization' – which is to say, it goes from the non-actualized structure of the virtual to its representation in the actual, or as Deleuze puts it, 'from the conditions of a problem to the cases of a solution,'[27] i.e., the asset, like any economic object, is a solution to a problem.

The synthetic asset, then, is of course not *wholly* virtual insofar as it is actual. But it is also nonetheless truly ontologically unique in that, by virtue of its partiality, it still has one foot, so to speak, in the virtual. Deleuze is therefore saying that the synthetic asset, as an instance of a virtual object, is that much closer, ontologically, in approximation to the virtual, and in this sense 'enjoys the double property of transcendence and immanence in relation to the [the actual].'[28]

This, then, is perhaps the most peculiar, even paradoxical, yet inherently radical feature of the virtual object: it is an object, yes, and therefore in part undeniably actual; but it is also only partially actual, insofar as it is part virtual, and therefore is not self-reflexive, not over-determined by its concept, not confined by its pre-representation, not fully an actualized self-consistent identity – and yet for all this *it does have an actualized being*. It is this part of the virtual object that is the immaterial structure to materiality, an immateriality that has not been materially predetermined.

This paradox of the partially actual that is also singular structure is indeed what we have been witnessing throughout in our examinations of the progressive differentiation of synthetic finance – already in our opening examination of its material properties in Essay One, then in more depth in our case study in Essay Two, and which we now encounter in its philosophical formulation in *DR* in Essay Three.

And Deleuze is encouraging us to take this thought a step further. For the latent but profound and monstrous power of the virtual object lies precisely in its fuzzy ontological, peculiar materiality. It is 'enough' in the virtual to retain its prior formative role in conditioning the structure to the morphogenesis of actuality, yet without being confined to the invariance requirements placed on the flat space of the actual. But it is also 'enough' in the actual to still be relatively accessible to thought, a thought that feeds back into structure, a solution that feeds back into problems, a not-fully determined actuality that conditions the condition of the actual itself.

Qualitative multiplicities

i. It is important to know that in *DR* Deleuze is constantly giving philosophical transformation to mathematical and scientific concepts. No Deleuzian concept better illustrates the rigors involving this practice than that of the multiplicity.

In his book on Bergson, Deleuze credits Riemann with discovering this concept (Riemann, our reader may or may not know, was the non-Euclidean geometer Einstein was reading during his *annus mirabilis* – when, closing-up the patent office for the night, he walked home to smoke his cheap tobacco and re-envision the (non-Euclidean) structure of the universe). Riemann immediately applied the concept of the multiplicity, or manifold, to study geometric spaces, or more broadly mathematical spaces. Physicists apply its concept to study physical spaces. Dynamical systems theorists apply it to study dynamical systems, or objects as systems. Because markets are dynamical systems, and assets are dynamical objects, we can apply the concept to study assets and the markets they populate.

Our examination of synthetic finance has revealed that any asset is dynamically composed of a formless mess of different properties, which can be plastically stripped and injected elsewhere, or created or destroyed ex nihilo, ad infinitum, and nonlinearly. Our case study and Deleuze have independently observed that if new and different economic properties constantly 'swarm in the fracture' of the repetition of the object, if they are 'constantly emerging on its edges, ceaselessly coming and going, being composed in a thousand different manners,'[29] then to speak of any given economic object as having an 'essence' is symptomatic of a bad ontology and its correlative ideology of what we labeled 'asset-fetishism.' And that to dispense with this, we should cease believing the asset *must* have some kind of fixed, inherent, or internalized essence. For the essence of any asset 'is nothing but an empty generality,' which means nothing apart from its many different economic properties.[30]

For this reason Riemann, Deleuze, and our speculative materialism agree that we are more justified to think of the object *qua* asset as a multiplicity. Simply put: a multiplicity is the term we use to denote the constitutive processes of an object. Multiplicities are the n-dimensional site for the process of their assembly – which 'is' a continuous becoming. This means that multiplicity is the concept used to denote a reality; in truth, an abundance of reality that is not always or only actual, not always or only virtual, not always or only potential; but rather a confluence of all three registers of reality, which is predicated on amounts, or degrees, and kinds of amounts of processes – whether intensive or extensive – that define the object.

Two questions immediately arise, which we will address herein.

First, what is the ontological status of the multiplicity? We have explicitly declared our concern with the ontology of economic objects throughout our Essays – and especially with the ontology of the synthetic asset. Let us first address this question.

Second, we have spoken throughout of the relation between the three classes of exchange (classical exchange, generic finance, synthetic finance); and we have observed that their respective objects (physical objects, generic assets, synthetic assets) populate different domains of action, or markets (flat space and curved space). So there is the question of what class of economic object has what kind of multiplicity?

ii. Let us address the first question by introducing our reader to the general ontology of multiplicities. If multiplicities denote the process of assembly of the object; and if as Deleuze, following Riemann, will show, multiplicities come in two varieties, what general processes characterize multiplicities in general?

To ask the question of what is the ontological status of the multiplicity is to ask the question of what is the ontology of the asset.

Every asset is a multiplicity. In particular, for Deleuze an asset 'is an n-dimensional, continuous, defined multiplicity.'[31] For this reason to propose to examine the asset as a multiplicity is to propose to examine the asset as a dynamical object – for every such object has n-dimensions, is continuous, and defined.

Let us break down this dense definition.

- By 'dimensions' Deleuze means 'the variables of coordinates' upon which the actualized phenomenon of the asset depends.

  Deleuze repeatedly observes throughout *DR* what we have independently stumbled upon time and again in our examination of synthetic finance: namely, to presume that because an exchange is ostensibly bilateral, it necessarily follows that the dimensions to the space of an exchange are flat, i.e., zero-curvatured, which is to say Euclidean, is not so much always wrong as only sometimes true. However, this is an analytical error that has grave political-economic consequences; more specifically, this is to error in underestimating what the economic object is capable of in the course of its transformation into its image of value as money – it is to restrict in our minds what the object is capable of in reality as it *repeats* itself in the course of moving from one to another place, *differently*, in space.

  As the economic properties which otherwise remain invariant in the exchange of flat space economic objects are loosened, as in a synthetic exchange, even dimension is not necessarily an invariant property of an exchange. This is to say that the variables of coordinates upon which the actualized asset depend can change, i.e., they are not invariant. Deleuze's point will be that far from this signaling the outbreak of all chaos for exchange, it is the condition of possibility for a nomadic distribution. This is also a truth upon which a wager or two of our own speculative materialism is predicated, and the rock on which our proposal for a universal synthetic CDO stands.

- By 'continuity' Deleuze means 'the set of relations between changes in these variables,' and which distribute the structure to its space of possibilities.

  If the variables of coordinates that distribute the structure to the space of possibilities of the properties of the asset can warp, bend, twist, or otherwise alter, so too can the relations between these variables. This of course does not mean that they must or necessarily will change in a radical or sudden manner. In fact, continuity first and foremost denotes the set of relations between the variables may only infinitesimally change; or else if not ostensibly changing in space, will appear to only change in time, e.g., a stationary apple that decomposes 'in time' eventually changes its spatial metrics; so too does a stationary wooden apple, albeit merely at a different rate.

  In fact, it is the case that if there is very little or even no ostensible change in variables of the coordinates of the asset, the asset will be capable of doing very little other than, like the apple that decomposes in time, growing or shrinking in its value – which is to say that the orientation of the object will change in space in the course of an exchange, but without that space being reoriented in any meaningful way. It is therefore always a matter of knowing whether the set of relations between the variables are capable of changing, and at what rhythm and rate, i.e., what is their spatial and temporal organization – and if so, what is their effect on the material properties of the asset? But there is also the question of what, if any, is the reciprocal effect of the movement of the asset on the structure of its space, or domain of action, i.e., its market?
- By 'definition' Deleuze means 'the elements reciprocally determined by these relations, elements which cannot change without the multiplicity changing its order and metric.'[32]

  We too have observed this theme throughout our examination of the ontology of financial assets: the 'elements,' as Deleuze calls them, are the economic properties constitutive of the asset.

  To say that these properties will not change without the asset changing its order and metric is simply one more way of observing, as we have, that the metrics, or what we called in Essay One the 'material properties' of the asset, can change in the course of its repetition, as in a synthetic exchange. We have seen that the generic asset is repeated by the synthetic asset, and in the course of its repetition the asset changes in kind, as new properties differentiate. We have also considered that, even before that, the generic asset was repeating the physical asset, and in the course of its repetition new properties (e.g., maturity, yield, default risk, etc.) differentiated as well.

  However, let us read this definition of 'definition' carefully. If the properties of the asset that are 'reciprocally determined' by the relations between the variables of coordinates of that asset cannot change without the asset changing both 'its order *and* metrics,' the question arises whether to change the metrics of the asset also necessarily changes its order? The answer to this question, as we have seen, is no, it does not: the repetition of the natural object by the classical object repeats the natural object, but in the course of

> its repetition preserves its identity – which is to say that it does not change in kind; the repetition of the classical object by the generic asset repeats the classical object, but in the course of its repetition preserves its identity as well – which is to say that it also does not change in kind. However, by contrast we have seen that the synthetic asset constitutes both a change to the metrical properties *and* the order of the multiplicity – it repeats, and in the process of repeating, produces a new difference *not only in degree, but a change in degree that produces a new difference in kind.*

From this, we immediately recognize that our question about the general ontology of the multiplicity is a question about causality, its nature and conditions. It is a question of exogenous and endogenous force. It is a question about the conditions of actuality, of the extrinsic structure to intensive determination and the intensive processes to extensive actualization. For this reason, to think the asset as a multiplicity is to think the continuous and simultaneous interpellation of forces acting both on it from without, and throughout it from within – its thousand, open, continuous plateaus of n-dimensional space, which disrupt our prejudices of an inside-outside distinction that holds. And most directly, to think the asset as a multiplicity is to convoke the question of change. For as Deleuze puts it:

> [The asset's] spatial dramatization is played out on several levels: in the constitution of an internal space, but also in the manner in which that space extends into the external extensity, occupying a region of it.[33]

The reason why this is the case, is simply that the asset is a living being. And as such:

> A living being is not only defined genetically, by the dynamisms which determine its internal milieu, but also ecologically, by the external movements which preside over its distribution within an extensity.[34]

iii. Let us then attend to our second question – of what kind of asset has what kind of multiplicity?

To begin, let us first consider two examples of an asset as a multiplicity. Let us consider the multiplicity of a classical object, a hot dog, and a generic financial asset, a Treasury bond.

We can imagine that over a period of weeks, and months, and even years, we literally sit and watch a hot dog age beyond its expiration date. It will progressively become inedible, begin to decompose, and eventually disintegrate into the ambient, surrounding space. What are we doing? We are watching the hot dog's motion through time. We are observing the physical motion of the hot dog in space, in time – in space-time.

Of course, while the hot dog is a natural object with a use value, it is also, and more importantly for us herein, an economic object, a physical commodity, or what we have called a classical object, in order to denote its classification in the group of exchange of classical exchange (let us ignore for the time being that a hot dog could be bought on credit; were this the case, the same logic of our point would apply – albeit now as a generic financial asset, which we discuss below). For this reason, when we see the natural object of the hot dog decompose in space-time, we are also seeing its metrics, or economic properties – in particular, the volume of its image of value – metamorphosize as well. And while we are not interested in the physical properties of the hot dog, per se, but rather in its economic or *material* properties (i.e., as an economic object), even if here it is the case that the physical properties of the object are tied to its material properties (a hot dog past its expiration date has little or no monetary value), most of us are surely willing to concede that (a) the cost of paint, paper, plastic, or pig parts affects the cost of the hot dog as an economic object, and (b) it is also the case that the former only matters, indeed is only economic and material, insofar as it is derived from and in itself for the latter. There is an apparent difference, then, yes, between a generic financial asset and a hot dog in that the tenure of the latter exchange is defined by immediate settlement, and so the image of value of the hot dog has little if any time to fluctuate over the course of the exchange. But the metrics of both the generic financial asset and the hot dog as an economic object are fully drawn from, or determined by, the broader, extrinsic, ambient space.

But now let us imagine that over a period of three months we sit and watch a 90-day Treasury bond age until it reaches maturity. And as we sit, watching, our eyes fixated on the document of the bond, in our peripheral vision we see the Federal Reserve pursue some quantitative easing, or relatedly, we see a rally in equities, or of hard or soft commodities, and so on; and we see what this does to the volume of the image of value of the bond. Here too, when sitting and watching the motion of the bond in space and time, we are observing the motion of the material properties – whether or not they are transformed – of the image of the object of the bond in space-time. We are observing the transformation of the economical object qua generic financial object under the force of motion of a domain of action that is, yes, bilateral (i.e., its exchange is ostensibly a bilateral transaction between two parties), but even more importantly still, is n-dimensional, continuous, and defined.

From this simple example, we see that the properties of a classical object and a generic financial asset both fully derive their metricization from the broader ambient economic space. At a most general level, this is entirely unsurprising for Deleuze's Riemann. For as Deleuze observes:

> Riemann defined as 'multiplicities' those things that could be determined in terms of their dimensions or their independent variables.

Riemann thus distinguished two kinds of multiplicities: there are what he called 'discrete multiplicities' and there are 'continuous multiplicities.' Their basic ontological distinction pivots on the manner of determination of their metrics:

> The former contain the principle of their own metrics (the measure of one of their parts being given by the number of elements they contain). The latter found a metrical principle in something else, even if only in the phenomena unfolding in them or in the forces acting in them.

Deleuze gives philosophical transformation to Riemann's original mathematical concept of the multiplicity. In the course of doing this, he deepens its ontological distinction.

There are, Deleuze agrees with Riemann, not one but two kinds of multiplicities: Deleuze re-labels 'discrete multiplicities' now as *numerical multiplicities*, and 'continuous multiplicities' now as *qualitative multiplicities* (he does this for reasons we will imminently discuss; we will henceforth defer to Deleuze's terminology).

Also like Riemann, Deleuze emphasizes as dispositive the manner of determination of their metrics. If the space of the multiplicity already contains the order of its metrics, rendering it uniform, fixed, with the distance between its points and lines being everywhere the same, then we know there will be very little or even no change between the variables of its coordinates, there will be very little or no change between the relations of these variables, and therefore there will be very little or no change to its properties: this is the case of a numerical multiplicity. The asset is repeated in the act of the exchange, but it is an invariable variation, an ex-change of the same.

But if the order of its metrics is determined by 'something else,' such as in 'phenomena' or 'forces' acting on or in and through them, in which case its metrics will *not* be fixed, flat, and uniform, and the distance between its points and lines will be uneven, contingent, and heterogeneous, then there is the capacity for change between the variables of its coordinates, there is the capacity for change between the relations of these variables, and there is very much a capacity for change to its properties, and radically so: this is the case of a qualitative multiplicity. Here, the asset is repeated in the course of its exchange, and a new difference in kind results.

Moreover, we will ultimately see that the profound ontological difference between these two kinds of multiplicities – the dispositive ontological difference that renders them irreducibly different in kind – *turns on the different functional relation between their material properties and the register of reality of their determination, or definition.*[35]

iv. Let us compare numerical multiplicities and qualitative multiplicities in more depth.

We first consider numerical multiplicities.

The object actualized by the numerical multiplicity is fully actualized, which we know because of the invariance requirements placed on its collinearities.

> In short, 'object' and 'objective' denote not only what is divided, but what, in dividing, does not change in kind. It is thus what divides by differences in

> degrees. The object is characterized by a perfect equivalence of the divided and divisions, of number and unit. In this sense, the object will be called a 'numerical multiplicity.' For number, and primarily the arithmetical unit itself, is the model of that which divides without changing in kind.

If classical economic objects, e.g., a hot dog, and generic financial assets, e.g., a 90-day Treasury bond, immediately appear to us as objectival, or at least 'more objective' than the synthetic asset, this distinction made by Deleuze helps to explain why. The flat object is chocked-full, phenomenally, with extensive economic properties – properties that divide, and in the course of their division, simply divide without changing in kind. Its properties are points on a line, and the points on the line are uniform, which means their division produces only changes by degrees, but no change in kind.

Already, for instance, in Essay One, when preliminarily concerning ourselves with the property of divisibility, we observed that the property of divisibility may turn out to be more than a matter of simple division. And that an interesting question convoked by the property of divisibility is not merely whether a particular financial asset can be divided, but whether it ever changes in kind when it does?

For example, in the matter of the division of a generic financial asset, we observed that if I receive a letter informing me that my round lot of Walt Disney Co. (DIS) stock has been divided, or 'split' 2-for-1, I will now own 200 shares at $25.00 per share, rather than 100 shares at $50.00 per share. Here there will have been the division of a generic financial asset, a division of 1 share of stock now into 2 – yet there will have been no change in kind, it has simply been numerically divided 'in half' or 'split' into two.

The same must be said of money. As the first generic financial asset, and perhaps finest example of a numerical multiplicity, money is the quintessential financial asset that divides without changing in kind. Deleuze observes that 'number has only differences in degree, or that its differences, whether realized or not, are always actual in it.'[36] In this respect, we realize that we could have invoked any number of examples of the division of a generic financial asset, for they are all numerical multiplicities. Whether a debt note, a loan, or money itself: we divide, and in the process of dividing there is no change in kind. Is a debt note available in an increment of a 100 dollars or 50? Does it matter? No – its yield will be the same. Is a loan syndicated? The answer to this question is a mere arithmetical formality. Do I 'break' a 100 dollar bill in order to get back five $20s, ten $10s, or a 100 $1s? Does it matter? No – the amount is unchanged by its denomination.

But let us now consider the qualitative multiplicity.

The qualitative multiplicity is much less defined in actuality, and therefore has far fewer invariance requirements on the collinearities preserved by flat space classes of exchange. Moreover, whereas in a numerical multiplicity the order of its metrics is already found in one of its parts – i.e., being extensive and uniform, everything is already contained in its matter, all or most of its reality has been presented to actuality – this is not so with a qualitative multiplicity.

> [A qualitative multiplicity] does not divide up without changing in kind, it changes in kind in the process of dividing up: This is why it is a nonnumerical multiplicity, where we can speak of 'indivisibles' at each stage of the division.[37]

It is true that our case study of synthetic finance in Essay Two was all along dealing with a qualitative multiplicity – and that this accounts for the radical loosening of invariance requirements on the collinearities in the synthetic exchange. For example, in the process of pooling and tranching a synthetically replicated portfolio of generic assets, we pooled and then re-divided the risk and cash flow, and in the process of re-dividing the risk and cash flow, we witnessed a change to the risk and cash flow in kind. Or even already in a single-name CDS, we stripped, i.e., 'divided' the event risk and associated cash flow from the generic referent – and in the process of its division, the terms of the preexisting generic financial exchange changed in kind.

Moreover – as we spoke of above in passing – Deleuze alerts his reader to the importance of understanding that a crucial ontological difference adheres between these two kinds of multiplicities. The dispositive ontological property rendering these two multiplicities irreducibly different in kind *turns on the different functional relation each multiplicity maintains between their specific material properties and the register of reality of their definition.*

For as Deleuze points out, on the one hand:

> Everything is actual in a numerical multiplicity; everything is not 'realized', but everything there is actual. There are no relationships other than those between actuals, and no differences other than those in degrees.[38]

But on the other hand:

> [The properties by which] a nonnumerical multiplicity … is defined, plunges into another dimension.… It moves from the virtual to its actualization, it actualizes itself by creating lines of differences that correspond to its differences in kind.[39]

What are these 'lines of difference' that the qualitative multiplicity 'actualizes' by virtue of partially 'plunging' its object into another dimension? What does this 'plunging' mean for the definition of the material properties of the asset to which the qualitative multiplicity corresponds?

In truth, we have already begun to address this question. Let us recall (please see 'Virtual Objects') that the radical potential of the virtual object resides in the paradoxical, hybridized dimensionality of its reality: it simultaneously inhabits two dimensions of reality as a virtual object, it has both one foot in the virtual, and one foot in the actual; it comprises a reality that paradoxically houses an object that is a mere shred of the actual, while yet also still possessing some of the non-substantive structure of the virtual.

The answer to these questions, then – of what are these 'lines of difference that correspond to its difference in kind?', and how does such 'hybridized reality affect the order of the asset's properties?' – according to Deleuze, is precisely what marks the peculiar but radical ontology of the qualitative multiplicity, and therefore the peculiar but radical materiality of synthetic finance, as such.

v. The radical materiality of the synthetic is best articulated by Deleuze, when outlining the three principal ontological features of the qualitative multiplicity. They are as follows:

(1) First, 'the elements [viz. properties] of the multiplicity have neither sensible form nor conceptual signification ... they imply no prior identity, no positing of something that could be called one or the same. On the contrary, their indetermination renders possible the manifestation of difference freed from all subordination.'[40]

This deepens the meaning of precisely what our own case study on credit derivatives has observed: the economic properties both actualized by the synthetic exchange and actualizing the synthetic asset imply no prior identity, they are free from the invariance requirements on the collinearities to which the classical object and generic asset are subordinated. Such 'indetermination' of the object means that the synthetic asset is lacking any predetermined economic 'form,' is free from predefined variables of its coordinates, as well as free of any predefined relations otherwise existing between them.

(2) Second, then, the properties and relations between the properties of the multiplicity are determined, reciprocally determined – as they are in all multiplicities, both numerical and qualitative. But now their determination occurs 'without external reference or recourse to a uniform space in which it would be submerged.'[41] The qualitative multiplicity is, as Deleuze puts it, 'intrinsically-defined.'[42]

If the invariance requirements on the collinearities and on so many other economic properties predefining the conditions of possibility for the behavior of flat space economic objects are capable of being loosened in a synthetic exchange, this is because the structure to the space of their qualitative multiplicity is not fixed, flat, uniform or homogeneous, i.e., it is not Euclidean. Rather, it is topological – which means that its surface is a space unto itself, and that space is not restricted by the collinearities. It is an intrinsically defined and fungible space, capable of warping, bending, twisting, folding over into or out of itself, or vanishing and suddenly reappearing. This also helps to explain why its mode of distribution is nomadic – it involves a distribution of space itself, rather than a distribution of objects in a pre-distributed space.

What, then, is the difference between the structures to the space of the markets populated by numerical and qualitative multiplicities, respectively? In short, the structure to the space populated by numerical multiplicities is a corrugated plane of sheet-metal, lain flat upon a zero-curvatured floor: its rigid objects move to and fro on its surface, symmetrically translating back and forth along its parallel ridges. And yet, really, what more can the non-fungible objects populating this flat space do than ex-change their position, or orientation, on this flat sheet now for an image of this or that position a little bit further ahead along the ridge? It is change, indeed, and technically speaking. But it is an empty change, an invariable form of variation, a transformation that involves no real change.

Contrarily, the structure to the space populated by qualitative multiplicities is an unbounded, elastic, soft cotton bed-sheet flipped up into the air, falling slowly through the air, and now down, down, down, towards an indefinite ground of indeterminate shape below. The surface of the bed-sheet and the ground below have yet to de-differentiate themselves, or become one, which they will and do at the moment when the bed-sheet touches ground. At the moment it touches the ground it will become metricized, striated, numerical. For now, though, the surface of the bed-sheet floats, suspended above the ground; it is a moving horizon, populated by fungible objects, and subject to an invisible force – indistinct yet very real streams of air-flows moving beneath and above and beside and between the ever-changing curvatured surface of the sheet, with its thousand plateaus of n-dimensional folds and subfolds. It yet remains an uneven surface. Its fungible objects move to and fro on its surface, but it is highly improbable such objects rigidly translate back and forth, as if running along parallel lines. Rather, they more likely warp and bend the space around them as they move along the open terrain, or perhaps they will warp and bend themselves; perhaps their hard motion will be impeded, or redirected by another object on top of the surface, or now even an object beneath the sheet itself; perhaps their motion is soft. Perhaps the object is acutely sharp, or has a sharp edge that will insert a 'cut' in the surface of the sheet as it rolls along its surface. Does this object now fall through the sheet? Does this hole now act as a new attractor for the other objects circulating around on the sheet? If it is cut, will the sheet continue to tear, with its basin of attraction evolving in mid-flight? Given that the sheet is unbounded, how can we know?

We see that to ask the question about the objects populating this kind of surface – 'what more can they do than this?' – is perhaps even now premature, for do we even yet know 'anything' they can do, to which there is yet 'more'?

We do know, at least, that the structure to this space is plastic and ambiguously pliable, which now avails both the fungible objects and their space whose flexible structure is capable of being remade by the motions of such objects with any final, flat, uniform structure. We at least know that this space and the objects populating it are ontologically marked by a profoundly augmented capacity for change.

(3) Deleuze observes that these two aforementioned features mark the ontology of the qualitative multiplicity simply because the qualitative multiplicity 'is a structure,' albeit a highly fungible, profoundly indeterminate, truly paradoxical kind of structure. It is, in Deleuze's words, 'a system of multiple,

non-localizable connections between differential elements which is incarnated in real relations and actual terms.'[43]

Throughout our examination of the ontology of exchange we have seen that the morphogenesis of any economic object occurs 'between the virtual and its actualization' – or in other words, it goes from the structure [of the virtual] to its incarnation, from the conditions of a problem to the cases of a solution.'[44] However, we have also seen that the synthetic asset is singularly unique from the other two classes of flat space objects in that it still has one foot in the virtual. Indeed, this is why Deleuze argues that the synthetic asset is the object ontologically closest in approximation to the virtual object – the latter of which, we will recall, 'enjoys the double property of transcendence and immanence in relation to [the actual].'[45]

If synthetic assets are indeed qualitative multiplicities, let us follow this logic to the result: that the historico-ontological progressive differentiation of synthetic finance signals the coming-into-being of a series of qualitative multiplicities, such as credit derivatives and other synthetically structured assets (e.g., synthetic CDOs), which now enjoy 'this double property' of both transcendence and immanence in relation to the preexisting, actualized set of numerical multiplicities, which in turn populate the domains of action, or markets, comprising the system of exchange we call finance capitalism, what does this mean? It can only mean that now the determinative or defining virtual structure to the morphogenesis of economic form is more open and available to us, and increasingly so, than ever before. If the virtual is indeed, as Deleuze says, pure structure without content, both the condition for and conditioning of a problem whose solution is always found in the actual; and if synthetic finance now differentiates itself in order to assume this role, we must understand synthetic finance as the still partially virtual domain – or at least the domain closest, ontologically, to the virtual – where actual economic solutions acquire the conditional structure to their problems.

If there is a single lesson to be learned, and if there is collective mind to learn it, we now realize that perhaps we were always proceeding ontologically backwards by looking for good solutions to badly posed questions. The correct course of proceeding, rather, is to pose the virtual question whose actual solution will always be pre-determinatively commensurate with the quality of its problem. In other words, we do not need new solutions to preexisting problems, we need to formulate new problems to preexisting solutions – for the solutions will repeat themselves, producing a new difference in kind. This, indeed, is why we have elected to pursue the *speculative* activity of finance, rooted in a *materialist* method, and committed to the universalism of *communism*: a speculative materialist communism.

For this same reason, we now end our essay by beginning with some questions. In this respect, we now commence our project by concluding with some wagers, some speculative materialist wagers. This means that what follows is an ending, yes, but it is also our beginning: and our beginning is an ending with problems.

What follows are some problems we wager as questions, some questions we wager as problems. They are speculative. They are materialist. The following are three wagers of speculative materialism.

Three wagers of speculative materialism

i. In Essay One we inaugurated our study of the ontology of synthetic finance by examining some material properties of synthetic finance. In Essay Two we pursued a case study of credit derivatives in order to closely examine the ontology of the synthetic asset. And in Essay Three we outlined the radical political-economic applications of Deleuze's philosophical treatment of the mathematico-scientific concepts of difference and repetition, in order to substantiate our claim of the radical historical-materialist significance of the progressive differentiation of synthetic finance for our economic system writ large.

Our Three Essays of Speculative Materialism have thus ascended up the scale of the progressive differentiation of the synthetic – first as *properties*, then as *assets*, and finally as *system*. It is only fitting that we craft our formulation of three wagers of speculative materialism consistent with this ascending order. What follows, therefore, are three topical wagers – first on properties, then on assets, and then on system.

Wager One. There is a profound material effect of the hyperfungible properties of the synthetic asset on the properties of the system itself.
Question. Given the topological mode of assembly of the properties of the synthetic asset, is there now no limit to its material capacities?

In the course of our analysis of the different ontological genera of numerical and qualitative multiplicities, we observed the material differences between the processes of assembling the properties of flat space economic objects and those of synthetic assets.

To begin with, when everything is extensive in the object, we know that it will have a closed set of properties, with a fixed and finite number of potential combinations: we saw that this was the case with numerical multiplicities, and that it defines the materiality of flat space economic objects. However, we also saw that qualitative multiplicities have any number of intensive properties that adhere to the object; and while real, they are not necessarily actualized in the object, which means that at any given point there is an unknown open set of potential combinations of such properties; and that consequently no exhaustive enumeration of its properties is possible. Here, every repetition opens the object to a potential new difference in kind, for its difference is neither subject to the invariance requirements placed on rigid objects, nor does it pledge any allegiance to the collinearities. Rather, it is a difference that is unbounded, topological, absolute: we saw that this is the case with qualitative multiplicities, and that it defines the materiality of the synthetic asset.

It is therefore neither hyperbolic nor metaphorical for us to observe that there are two modes of assembling the properties of an economic object. And yet because there has hitherto been no political-economic conceptual distinction drawn between different modes of objectival composition – that is, until now – we must both hyperbolize and draw on metaphor to exposit these two distinct modes of assembly.

There is (a) an industrial-line or mechanical mode of assembly, and (b) a biological mode of assembly: these modes of assembly are qualitatively different, and each of their respective objects has kinds of material properties endemic to its mode of assembly.[46] Let us consider them.

(a) In a mechanical assembly-line, the constitutive properties of the object are uniform, fixed, finite, i.e., Euclidean. The static order and rigid metrics of its shapes, sizes, lengths, values (of angles, etc.), and other material properties remain invariant under their predetermined motion along the assembly-line. The component parts of the object move along conveyor belts and other standardized transport facilities, in order to be exactly positioned relative to each other. Indeed, *they must necessarily* be precisely arranged, as such, for their viable composition.

(b) By contrast, in a biological mode of assembly, topological properties define the dynamical order and plastic metrics that intrinsically unfold in its parts. Herein, fungibility is the order of the day: for example, specific lengths of muscles are less important than their attachments points – the muscles will bend or warp to fit the bone; the shape of membranes are less relevant than their continuity and closure – diffusion processes allow for flexible adaptability, as is needed; cellular components do not require exact positioning – they float around, using lock-and-key mechanism to find their match.[47]

Our reader by now well knows that synthetic exchange is isomorphic to a biological mode of assembly. The only question is whether, given its topological propensities, there is any endogenous limit to its material capacities?

An expanded version of our first wager can thus be formulated, accordingly: we may, in fact, not need a wholesale simultaneous systemic mutation to yield a viable new order and its metrics – as a mechanical assembly-line mode of thinking about (r)evolution has always presupposed. In fact, a simple lock-and-key mechanism is not only more than capable of flexibly restructuring the intrinsically unfolding parts, and their constitutive relations between variables; rather this may turn out to be the *only* effective method by which to yield systemic change.

Wager Two. There will be uneven effects of sedentary uses of nomadic technologies, because nomadic technologies must be used nomadically.
Question. Is the nature of the synthetic asset at odds with its current uses? If so, what is its effect on system?

In *DR*, Deleuze illustrates that extensive differences are expressed in the actual as the negation of differences; such differences are what we call 'diversity' – i.e., that some-*thing* is not some-*thing else* negates their intensive, positive differences; and then we assert that only diverse things are negatively alike, and by virtue of their diversity. But that contrarily, intensive differences are positive differences, and such positive differences in any dynamical system can reach a critical threshold, in which an incremental change by degrees can actualize a radical, qualitative, material change in kind (e.g., thermodynamics is the original field of study of the effects of intensive differences, for instance between pressure and temperature in one and the same body, that, reaching a critical threshold, will cause a dynamical reaction, thus changing the body in kind).

From this, it seems we have a ready-made, highly compelling question to pose about the conditions of possibility for financial crisis. Are positive differences made intense enough with the advent of synthetic finance so as to have now reached a critical threshold, in which our financial system is undergoing a radical qualitative change to its order and metrics – i.e., from a static equilibrium, wherein differences are dampened or cancelled, to now a state of non-equilibrium, wherein differences remain – paradoxically – both interiorized yet actual, both virtual and extensive? But perhaps this is merely to ask whether the seemingly ever-present progressively intensified instability of our financial system is now a profound symptom that, given the increasing use of synthetic assets to always play a zero-sum game (i.e., whereby the house wins, or the gambler wins, but never both), their use today, as such, is anathema to their nature?

Here we are immediately reminded of the important ontological distinction drawn by Deleuze between sedentary distribution – a dividing up of that which has already been distributed – and nomadic distribution – which is a 'completely other distribution … without property, enclosure or measure … a space which is unlimited, or at least without precise limits.'[48] Deleuze, so far as we know, does not hazard to guess what happens when a technology original to nomadic distribution is repeatedly deployed for sedentary purposes. But this is precisely what is at stake today: whether the nature of the synthetic asset is at odds with its current uses? And if it is, what is its effect on the financial system?

An expanded version of our second wager thus follows: insofar as intensive differences drive fluxes of matter and energy (realized as either the migratory movements of a given population, or movements of energy through a given population), and insofar as the objects of synthetic finance, as qualitative multiplicities, are marked by a quantitative increase of intensive differences, the proliferation of systemic instability is an acute symptom of the sedentary misuse of a nomadic technology. Is not the only way to preserve system-viability to change the system's sedentary distribution, to cease using a nomadic technology as a sedentary technology? Is not the only way to maintain the concept of profitability to now achieve universal equitability – that for the first time in the history of humanity, we our brought to a place whereby the equitable is the most profitable? And failing in the achievement of the equitable, profitability will falter as well?

Wager Three. Capital is the original topological invariant. Synthetic finance allows us to increasingly access its intensive properties. Capital is gaining symmetry, not losing it.
Question. What, if any, is the historical-materialist systemic significance of the regressive differentiation of the economic object?

Natural studies on symmetry illustrate the process by which differentiated structures progressively emerge as any given dynamical system or object develops. There is a qualitative difference between the undifferentiated abyss of indetermination and those progressively defined, increasingly distinctive zones of concentration and established polarities of position that always actualize by way of symmetry-breaking events.[49] For example, modern neuroscience speaks of the self-amplifying fluctuations in synaptic density from an initially undifferentiated and spatially disordered brain, productive of the broken symmetry that results in neurocentral organization. Microbiologists studying the aggregation of slime-mold stress the importance of symmetry-breaking and entrainment for the progressive actualization of a multicellular organism. Embryological research on egg-fertilization emphasizes the organizational work of cleavage patterns, transforming a highly symmetric ooze into differentiated tendons and muscles, blood, brain, and bones. Cosmologists model the expansion-to-cooling phase of our universe to gain insight into the symmetry-breaking bifurcations that allowed for the differentiation of our basic physical forces (at extreme high temperatures precipitating the birth of our universe, the four forces were yet one). Even geologists studying hydrological patterns are delighted to observe pattern-generating asymmetries of river-formation, as the dynamical flow of water bifurcates, inscribing its sculptures into the face of our Earth.

What repetition threads through the multitude of differences of these phenomena? On the one hand, there is no shortage of corroborating evidence from the science of morphogenesis that the metrical structures of such systems differentiate through a cascade of symmetry-breaking phase transitions – as if all itemized actuality is the result of emergence from yet some virtual and undifferentiated, nonmetricized, topological space. And yet, on the other hand, they all concede that the price paid for a structure of order is the loss of white symmetry, an accruement of the burden of rigidity, a diminution in genetic fungibility – as if, in turn, a kind of fee charged by Charon for safe passage from the virtual to the actual across the river of potentiality is a renunciation of primal pliability, and the only accepted currency broken symmetry herself.

From one angle, and provisionally, one might expect that the historical differentiation of synthetic finance from out of generic finance, and before that, of generic finance from out of classical exchange, will have followed a linear, straightforward, morphogenetic narrative of the progressive differentiation of our system of finance capitalism along this familiar storyline of symmetry-breaking at the origins and development of metricized structure. But our ontological approach to the study of finance quickly showed us that in fact the opposite is true. Yes, a topological space will differentiate itself, dividing its continuity, becoming progressively rigid, metricized, and inflexible as it undergoes a cascade of symmetry-breaking events. But how then do we account for more symmetry, more fungibility, and less-differentiation marking the historically more recent synthetic financial asset and its correlative class of exchange?

An expanded version of our third wager can therefore be formulated in the following manner: remarkably and quite unexpectedly but undeniably today, *beneath the historical and ostensibly linear progressive differentiation of finance, we are witnessing the ontological regressive differentiation of capital –and now especially in its synthetic-systemic incarnation.* From an originally more metricized, geometrically homogeneous, and flat economical space populated by rigid economic objects, we are now *regressing forward* towards a less metricized, more fungible, and topological economical space populated by synthetic objects.

This is truly an exciting moment, indeed. And for this very reason, let us note that one of the tasks – if not *the* principal task – of the speculate materialist is to search out and locate those indistinct zones, or areas, from the world of finance where the virtual is still discernible without being determined, still expressed without its expression yet covered-over, its intensive properties articulated but not yet extensively cancelled-out. For it is here, in studying such areas of our dynamical system, we will discover how to better seize the flexible, fungible, formative, monstrous and nomadic power of qualitative multiplicities. Of course, we now know that synthetic finance is a good place to start, for it is precisely such an area. Indeed, it is the area par excellence.

Notes

1 *Difference & Repetition* is the greatest of all books of philosophy. However, it is quite *difficult* to fully grasp because Deleuze presumes, or even demands, a working understanding of many mathematical and several scientific fields of study (e.g., group theory, non-Euclidean geometry, calculus, topology, a little biology and physics, and dynamical systems theory). It is also quite *dense* because Deleuze 'zips-up' these various discourses into a compressed, cohesive whole. But it is ultimately very *rich* because it draws out the deep ontological significance – as only a great book of philosophy can – of their combined mathematical and scientific insights, i.e., of Galois, Riemann, Leibniz, Curie, Einstein, and so on: as if they were able to sit in a room, discussing a pure ontology among themselves, but now equipped with a (Deleuzian) language to streamline their collective discourse.
2 *DR* p. 57.
3 Ibid. p. 128.
4 Ibid. p. 24. (Note: 'the Idea' is Deleuze's present term herein for a qualitative multiplicity which we discuss below – please see 'Qualitative Multiplicities'.)
5 Ibid. p. 2.
6 Ibid. p. 24.
7 Ibid. p. 24.
8 Ibid. p. 169.
9 Ibid. p. 182.
10 Ibid. p. 67.
11 Ibid. p. 67.

12 Ibid. p. 69.
13 Ibid. p. 25.
14 Ibid. p. 36.
15 Ibid. p. 36.
16 Ibid. p. 36.
17 Ibid. p. 37.
18 Ibid. p. 29.
19 While *actuality* is that which is actual to the senses (or what we colloquially, if mistakenly, call 'reality'), and *potentiality* is that which is possible, and therefore subject to a probability distribution, *virtuality* is that register of reality which structures the space of what is possible to become actual.
20 *DR* p. 100.
21 Ibid. pp. 100–101.
22 Ibid. p. 102.
23 Ibid. p. 102.
24 Ibid. p. 101.
25 Ibid. pp. 208–209.
26 Ibid. p. 102.
27 Ibid. p. 183.
28 Ibid. p. 189.
29 Ibid. p. 169.
30 Ibid. p. 182.
31 Ibid. p. 182.
32 Ibid. p. 182.
33 Ibid. p. 216.
34 Ibid. p. 216.
35 By 'definitions' we wish to denote the full aforementioned Deleuzian meaning of the term. This is another way of observing that the ontological difference between numerical and qualitative multiplicities turns on their different 'kinds' of symmetry – that while classical symmetry marks the numerical multiplicity, a secondary, apparently discordant, or even ostensibly 'derivative' kind of symmetry (but which is a symmetry nonetheless – and at that, a more ontologically fundamental symmetry) marks the qualitative multiplicity.
36 Gilles Deleuze, *Bergsonism*, Zone Books, 1988, p. 41.
37 Ibid. p. 42.
38 Ibid. p. 43.
39 Ibid. p. 43.
40 *DR* p. 183.
41 Ibid. p. 183.
42 Ibid. p. 183.
43 Ibid. p. 183.
44 Ibid. p. 183.
45 Ibid. p. 189.
46 There are at least two texts to visit whose authors note this distinction, albeit with different language. See Manuel De Landa, *Intensive Science and Virtual Philosophy*, Continuum, 2002, esp. pp. 66–67, and from whom we draw this distinction; and Gilles Deleuze and Felix Guattari, *A Thousand Plateaus: Capitalism & Schizophrenia*, University of Minnesota Press, 1987, esp. chapter 9.
47 De Landa p. 66.
48 Ibid. p. 36.
49 J. Maynard Smith and G. Vida (eds.), *Organizational Constraints on the Dynamics of Evolution*, Manchester University Press, 1990; F. Yates *et al.* (eds.), *Self-Organizing Systems: The Emergence of Order*, Plenum Press, 1987.

Appendices

Two kinds of symmetry, three classes of exchange

Appendix 1 – Symmetry and exchange (or, economic transformations)

i. In Essay One we inaugurated an examination of the ontology of synthetic finance. In Essay Two we pursued a case study on credit derivatives to deepen our understanding of this ontology. In Essay Three we finished by outlining the speculative materialist wagers of synthetic finance. This warrants some abstraction to the concepts endemic to our method, and as related to our wagers, derived from our case study, and predicated on our opening investigation into the material properties of synthetic finance. This is the purpose of the Appendices.

ii. We know that to study synthetic finance is to study a group of transactions comprising a class of exchange, which is a subclass of the more general class of exchange labeled 'finance.' In turn, to study finance is to study a group of transactions comprising a class of exchange, which is a subclass of the total classes of exchange we call 'exchange.'

But what does it mean to study exchange? The short answer is that it is to study the operation of a commensurability or equivalence between an economic object and its image of value as money; for without such operation, the object will remain where it is, insofar as no price will be agreed to, and no exchange will occur. All subsequent economic developments and discourses – e.g., in technologies, distributions of resources, of markets and their objects, the materializations of formal and informal institutions, and so on – are implicitly predicated on this first fact.

If we are then willing to agree that exchange, fundamentally, is the transformation of an object into its image of value as money as it moves from one to another place in space, the first concept of concern for any examination of the ontology of exchange must be the operation of symmetry. Anytime we propose to study exchange, we are also proposing to study, whether we are aware of it or not, the operation of symmetry.

Group theory is the mathematical study of groups. Dynamical systems theory is the scientific study of the dynamics of complex systems. Both of these fields share in common with us a definition of symmetry.

By 'symmetry' we mean *invariance to change*. This means that the symmetry of an object, system, or motion is measured by the number of transformations which leave a property of that object, system, or motion invariant to change. This also means that symmetry is not a 'thing' or 'object,' per se, but insofar as it is an operation, is a procedural property of the transformation itself.

iii. From this, for us, two points follow.

First, while price is an extensive property of every act of exchange, symmetry is a quality of every act of exchange.

By this we mean that the representation of a certain *quantity* of symmetry is achieved in every money-mediated act of exchange, as the economic object is transformed into its image of value as money – and that this is represented in and as the object's price. But also that a certain *quality* of symmetry infuses every money-mediated act of exchange, for in the process of any given act of exchange achieving its quantity of symmetry, any number of economic properties of the object will remain *invariant* under the force of its transformation. So while it is the case that lacking symmetry, no price will be agreed to and no exchange will occur, it is also a matter of knowing which economic properties of the object do and do not remain invariant under the transformation we call exchange, which is to know both the quantity of symmetry in the act of its exchange, as well as the quality of symmetry marking its class of exchange.

To know both of these things is to know the structure to the space of transformation, or its 'domain of action,' which in economics we call a 'market'; and from this we then know any given economic object's equivalence class of exchange – which defines the invariance requirements of its space of transformation. For this reason, we will end our Appendices by inaugurating an examination of the concept denoting the spatiotemporal structures to different classes of exchange – we begin to consider markets as multiplicities.

We have said we are employing the group-theoretic mathematical definition of symmetry; but we have done this only after our own study of synthetic finance independently stumbled on to its concepts and methodology, and only insofar as they proved isomorphic to our own observation of the different invariance requirements placed on economic properties by different acts of exchange. In the gradual course of our research we began to realize that political economy has no reason to distinguish the economic concept of symmetry from its other mathematical, scientific, or aesthetic discursive usages. In studying exchange, it is not that we are *analogizing* economic objects to geometric figures (math), particles (physics), or icons on a column (aesthetics). Rather, by studying symmetry these fields concern themselves with a reality whose ontology is universal and isomorphic to them all. Colloquially, our reader may be prepared to agree. However, it is also a matter of knowing what exactly this entails.

Second, then, symmetry is also a quality of every class of exchange.

Once again, while we have applied, in this instance, a dynamical systems-theoretic understanding of symmetry, it is only after our own case study of synthetic finance independently stumbled on to its concepts and methodology; and only insofar as these proved isomorphic to our own observation that acts of exchange are dynamical processes, and that the progressive differentiation of any class of exchange is marked by a set of increasingly loosened invariance requirements on the properties of its objects, while yet always preserving a quantity and quality of symmetry nonetheless.

Let us consider this. If every act of exchange achieves symmetry, but any two given acts of exchange can have different amounts, this means that all acts of exchange are arrangeable into different classes of exchange. These classes *in toto* comprise a principal component of the interrelated dynamical system of economies we call 'the economy' – with all of its mobile institutions and moving horizon of markets, as well as the many varieties of classical, generic, and synthetic objects populating them, and in turn whose veritable dynamical properties are perpetually coming into and out of existence.

We have then noticed something puzzling, here. Natural studies on symmetry from the science of morphogenesis have long-illustrated the various processes by which the differentiated structures of any given dynamical system progressively emerge. We know that there is a qualitative difference between, on one side of reality, the undifferentiated abyss of a pre-actualized, purely symmetrical zone of indetermination, and on the other side, those progressively defined, increasingly distinctive zones of concentration that always actualize by way of symmetry-breaking events. Quite remarkably, a historical overview of the science of morphogenesis will observe so many repetitions of this same phenomenon in radically different registers:[1] all such studies illustrate that the metrical structures of a dynamical system differentiate through a cascade of symmetry-breaking phase transitions – as if the whole of itemized actuality is the result of an emergence from some virtual and undifferentiated, nonmetricized, topological space. And yet all such studies also reveal that the price paid for a structure of order is the loss of this primal symmetry, an incremental or sudden accruement of the burden of rigidity, a diminution in genetic fungibility – as if in turn a kind of fee charged by Charon for safe passage from the virtual to the actual across the river of potentiality is a renunciation of supple plasticity, the only currency accepted being broken symmetry herself.

When we are studying the historical development of finance from out of generic finance, and before that generic finance from out of classical exchange, what are we doing if not studying the progressive differentiation of the dynamical system of different spaces of exchange that we call *markets*? And what is transformed into their image of value from one to another place in the space of such markets if not the *economic objects* qua commodities we call classical objects, generic assets, and synthetic assets – each of which has progressively differentiated from its historically prior incarnation of the latter?

And yet how is it, then, as we asked at the end of Essay Three, that the progressive differentiation of generic finance from out of classical exchange, and then again synthetic finance from out of generic finance, actualizes a system whose materiality is marked by a *quantitatively augmented* and *qualitatively different* symmetry, with now also a *hyperfungibility*? Is the metricization of finance capital emerging, evolving or involving, and proliferating from out of the system of markets we call the economy, while yet also capital as finance is simultaneously *regressively differentiating*? Is capital differentiating itself to topology? And if so, what does this mean for the future of such a system and its material capacities?

iv. For this reason, our ongoing speculative materialist concern with symmetry in exchange is twofold.

First, we are concerned to know more about the general ontology of exchange. Our three Essays already alerted us to the peculiar materiality exhibited by the synthetic asset – with all its fungible and plastic properties that are uniquely createable, destroyable, injectable, extractable, distributable, and redistributable on a mobile horizon of dynamical processes. Our three Essays have already inaugurated an examination of the ontology of exchange, which we now must pursue further through a conceptual development of our method – a method whose first concept is the quantity or *degree* of symmetry achieved between any economic object (classical, generic, or synthetic) and its image of value as money; and the quality, or *kind* of symmetry marking its respective class of exchange (classical, generic, synthetic). We are interested in degrees of symmetry and kinds of symmetry – and especially the question of how it is that in the course of the progressive differentiation of finance, as in any dynamical system, we see a seemingly incremental move by degrees until finally there is produced a new change in kind?

In this respect, second, to inquire into the ontology of exchange is to inquire into the historical-materialist development of the classes of exchange that comprise the total group of automorphisms of exchange. For this reason our speculative materialist examination of the ontology of exchange will also eventually require a more comprehensive historical examination of the progressive differentiation of the different classes of exchange: from the historically first class of exchange that is classical exchange, to the progressive differentiation of generic finance from out of classical exchange, to now the progressive differentiation of synthetic finance from out of generic finance.

Assuming we can observe a historical trajectory to the nonlinear actualization of these three classes of exchange, should we not then also be able to sketch a rough outline of the topology of our differentiated system of exchange?

These are two important future objectives of speculative materialism. This is a wager on our method to keep in mind as we proceed.

Appendix 2 – Classical exchange

i. We commenced Appendix 1 by observing that, historically, synthetic finance is a subclass of the more general class of exchange labeled 'finance,' and that finance is a subclass of the total classes of exchange we call 'exchange.' We closed Appendix 1 by observing an isomorphism between any dynamical system and the dynamical system of finance, insofar as they involve transformations that involve the operation of symmetry, as an object is transformed into its image from one to another place in space.

A simple example from geometry already illustrates this truth.

Classical geometry studies the motions and properties of geometric figures in Euclidean space. For example, a triangle has a number of different properties (Figure A.1):[2]

- its shape
- the values of its angles
- the lengths of its sides
- its number of sides
- its perimeter
- its area (in 2-dimensions) or volume (in 3-dimensions)
- its separation into an inside and outside region
- its smell
- its color
- its position, or orientation, relative to some fixed axes in a surrounding space

The question is, which of these are to be considered *geometric* properties, and which of them are not?

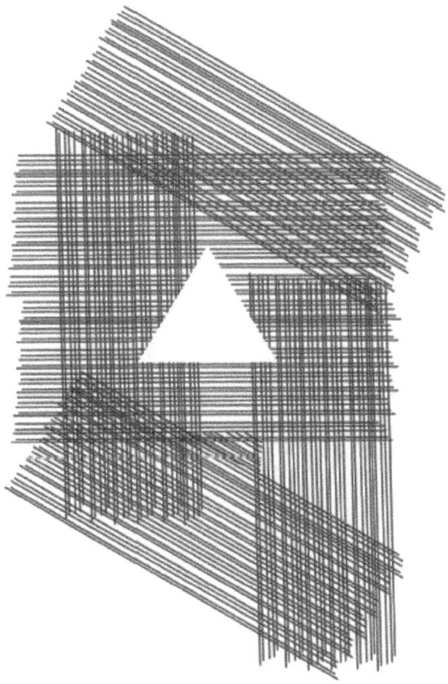

Figure A.1 Equilateral triangle.

Because the original answer to this question was given by classical geometry, it relied on a certain conception of symmetry, which is the classical conception of symmetry. In turn, classical symmetry relies on a certain conception of space, which is Euclidean space.

It seems obvious to us that neither smell nor color are geometric properties. However, what about the last property on the list – the property of position, or orientation, of the figure relative to some fixed axes in its surrounding space? Is orientation a geometric property?

To answer this question, classical geometry moves the figure from one to another place in space (Figure A.2); when the figure is moved, the geometer says, 'it has undergone a transformation into its image' (or sometimes, 'it has been transformed into itself'). Now, if the space of transformation is Euclidean, this space is flat and not curved, and the distance between its points and lines are fixed, regular, and everywhere the same. So when the figure has been transformed from one to another place in Euclidean space and now into its image, we see that all properties of the figure remain invariant under this change – that is, except the property of orientation. The figure's shape, its angles, lengths, its number of sides, perimeter, area, and separation of inside-outside have all

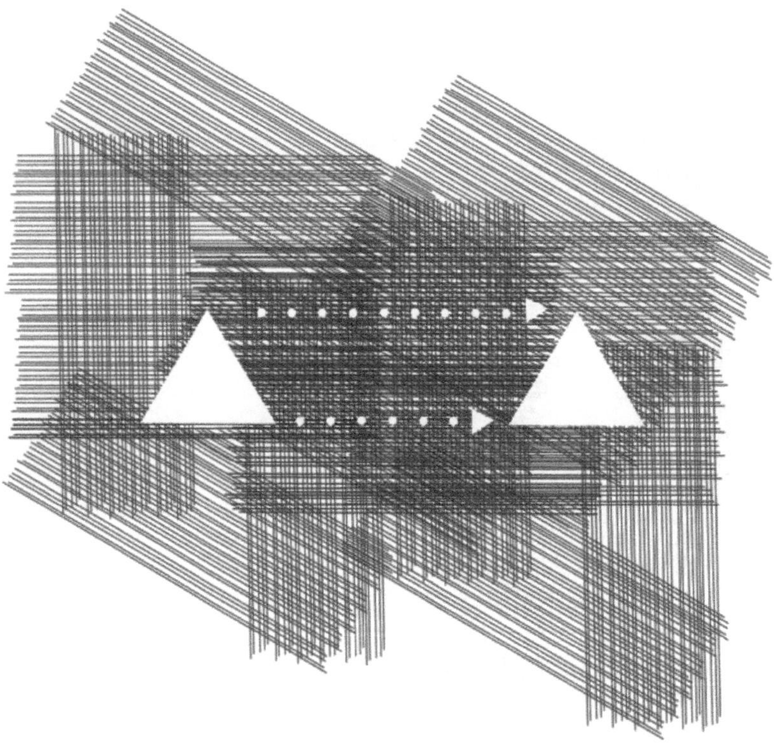

Figure A.2 Congruent transformation.

remained unchanged; but now the orientation of the figure relative to some fixed axes in its surrounding Euclidean space has changed.

Classical geometry reasons that because orientation is a property that is not invariant to change, it is therefore not a geometric property. And the next step in its logic follows: geometric properties are the properties of a figure that remain invariant to change when that figure is transformed into its image from one to another place in space. Because all of the geometric properties of all figures in Euclidean space remain invariant under their force of motion, every figure is congruent to itself when it is transformed into its image.

For this reason, the original class of motions of classical geometry are called *congruent motions*: a figure is congruently transformed into its image when it moves from one to another place in Euclidean space. Likewise, all figures that are congruent to themselves when reoriented in Euclidean space comprise an equivalence class of figures – a congruence class of geometric figures. And so if our equilateral triangle is always regarded as incongruent to a circle, square, any other triangle, or any other geometric figure, it is because they belong to different equivalence classes of geometric figures.

Let us consider this more fully.

We see that classical geometry implicitly uses our same *definition* of symmetry as invariance to change; but because its space of transformation is Euclidean, its *conception* of symmetry presumes a number of things about the behavior of the geometric properties of the figure when it moves about and ultimately into its image: it presumes that congruent motions are the only possible motions, or in other words that every figure will always remain congruent to itself when transformed into its image; and that therefore congruence is the only possible kind of symmetry transformation for a geometric figure.

For example, because the transformation of the figure is always a congruent motion, and because that figure always remains congruent to itself when transformed into its image, the geometric property of its area or volume will not grow or shrink over the course of the transformation; the lengths of its sides will not extend or contract, its number of sides will not multiply or divide; its shape will not stretch, twist, warp, or bend (Figure A.3); there will be no cut along its perimeter that suddenly de-differentiates or re-differentiates its inside from outside; and so on. Euclidean space is flat and not curved, and the distance between its points and lines are fixed, regular, and everywhere the same; so the motions to the transformation of the figure into its image *necessarily* appear to be congruent, and congruence will thus *necessarily* preserve all properties of the figure as it moves about in space.

But if we look closely, we see that the trick here is that already a property of the figure actually *has* changed with the motions of congruence – namely, its orientation in space (Figure A.2). Albeit classical geometry makes an original ontological decision to surreptitiously loosen an invariance requirement that otherwise *could have* been imposed on the property of orientation, had classical geometry decided to maintain an even more restricted conception of symmetry. But this would have involved an *absolute* invariance to *any* spatial

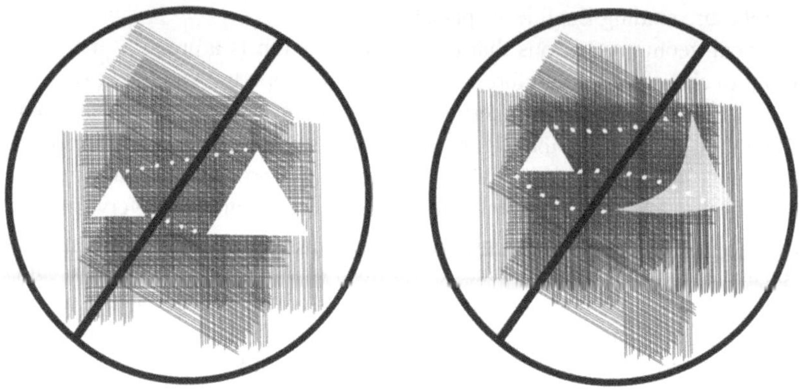

Figure A.3 What congruence does not allow.

change, insofar as to reorient the figure from one to another place in space does constitute *some* variance, i.e., there is a change to one of its original properties – namely, orientation. However, by electing to define orientation as a property, yes, but *not as a geometric property*, classical geometry from the outset makes a profound ontological decision, with profound material consequences. Classical geometry chooses not to distinguish between different figures that are oriented in different places in space, so long as their other properties – their geometric properties – are congruent: they are all regarded as belonging to the same equivalence classes if the geometric figures and their images are symmetrical to themselves; but they are regarded as belonging to different equivalence classes if the geometric figures and their images are not symmetrical to themselves.

Our reader can surely see why this decision to loosen the invariance requirement on orientation was necessary. Reorientation surely is a very important type of change. For if we take this thought a step further, it is hard to see how there could be *any* motion of *any* geometric figure whatsoever which did not preserve its identical orientation in space, if the invariance requirement on the property of orientation was not so loosened to begin with. Were this not the case, it would amount to classical geometry backhandedly proposing that any geometrical change to a figure whatsoever is impossible – i.e., that for all time geometric figures must remain in their same coordinated position, that their being will identically persist perpetually and forever in their same place, that no motion will ever occur, no spatial change will ever endure, and that *being in actuality*, as such, will be always simply be.

But this is not the case. We know that symmetry is not the same thing as absolute identity, sameness, or being without becoming, being always unchanging, or being ever unchanged. Rather, symmetry *requires some change* insofar as it always involves *an invariance under conditions of change*. For this very reason, we know the classical geometric conception of symmetry as congruence already *does* loosen one invariance requirement – i.e., the orientation of the figure relative to some fixed axes in surrounding space – while yet still regarding the figure as congruent and symmetrical to itself when transformed into its image from one to another place in space. Likewise, we see that there is more to symmetry than simply defining it as 'invariance to change,' or proposing to measure the symmetry of an object, system of objects, or motion by the properties which remain invariant to change. For already – unless we are asserting an absolute invariance on the orientation of actualized being, ubiquitous, incessant, and perpetual for all time – we must concede that *some* property will experience *some* change; and then it is simply a matter of deciding which properties, of how many properties, of knowing what is their space of transformation, and what is their symmetry group, or equivalence class?

For this reason as well, the study of the classical conception of symmetry is a first concept of concern for our speculative materialism when examining the ontology of exchange.

ii. We know that the earliest and oldest conception of geometric transformations belong to the class of motions labeled *congruent motions*. It is therefore no surprise to see that historical records inform us that the earliest and oldest practices of exchange belong to the group of transactions comprising the class of exchange we call *classical exchange*.

As far back as the early Stone Age, in the Paleolithic era, humanity was already exchanging jewelry and other goods according to rules dictated by tradition. At this young stage in the development of human economic institutions, there was still no defined concept of property, no method of preserving labor, only very primitive divisions of labor, and little if any specialized professions; there were no settled dwellings, few social connections outside of blood relations, but even the family was not yet a stable unit; there was only occasional and incidental production for the purposes of surplus, no taming or breeding of animals, no cultivation of plants, and widespread beliefs in magic permeated much of existence.

Indeed Heichelheim, who is our authority here, observes: 'the Paleolithic [era] presents for us a picture of an economic state of man which is lower in resources than at any time.'[3] However, notably there was already an exchange of objects; and there were already primitive forms of money acting as 'stand-in' images of value for one or more objects of exchange. For this reason, exchange in the Paleolithic era provides us with a good example of the group of congruent motions comprising the class of exchange of classical exchange – a class of exchange that to be sure still remains, and is no less prevalent today.

Heichelheim documents the practical problems in achieving economic symmetry that culminated in Paleolithic exchange by way of money. 'Pure barter,' as he puts it, often entailed a long and painstaking search for objectival equivalence until finally both parties to the exchange were able to find goods they found useful and satisfactory, and in commensurable quantities:

> Consequently, society soon began, perhaps as early as the Paleolithic stage, to give preference to certain wares, which were desirable to all from religious or economic reasons. These are the beginnings of money ...[4]

Heichelheim observes the varieties of materials used as money ('which varies according to tribe and locality, and takes the form of plates of ostrich shells, shellfish, lumps of salt, bracelets or chains of conventional designs and material, pearls of all kinds, stones of every form, boar's tusks, elephant's tusks, or dog's teeth'), and the varieties of goods bought and sold therein (whether with 'tools money,' 'food money,' 'clothes money,' certain 'decorative axes,' and so on).[5] It seems that early Stone Age moneys – which would later, as a more generalized money-form, achieve the status of a singular, formal, universal equivalent form of value, i.e., as these different types of moneys over time began to regressively de-differentiate themselves into simply 'money' – while evidently not yet universal, from the beginning spontaneously assumed the power to actualize the property of symmetry by numerically representing, in imagistic form, the values of dissimilar quantities of qualitatively distinct objects.

It is difficult to overstate the radical impact of this ontological development, i.e., of the simultaneous movement of the progressive differentiation of moneys, as a power of converting into numerical images the measurable values of various economic objects, while also regressively de-differentiating themselves in order to increasingly assume the rarified status of one universal equivalent – e.g., of streamlining exchange, of opening up its portal of liquidity, of offering itself as a stand-in substitute for economical objects with their images of value.

However, and importantly for our understanding of the invariance requirements marking classical exchange, we must also observe here that while Paleolithic money-mediated exchange involved the reorientation of an object as it was transformed into its image of value, it otherwise maintained very restrictive invariance requirements on the other economic properties of all objects exchanged.

For example, we know that (Figures A.4a and A.4b):

(a) First, money used in Paleolithic exchange was 'only used for certain purposes [insofar as] it could not be invested with interest, and [therefore] had only a limited economic value.'[6] This means that the image of value of the object was not allowed to fluctuate in any way – i.e., to neither appreciate nor depreciate – over the tenure of the exchange. And consequently, there was as yet no differentiated economic property of periodic yield, defined as interest rate.

(b) And second, this is the case because the tenure of the exchange was always restricted to immediate settlement. Indeed, if settlement in classical exchange is always immediate, there will *of course* be no economic property of interest rate, since such property has not yet differentiated itself from simple one-time yield or cash flow.

Figure A.4a Instance of classical exchange.

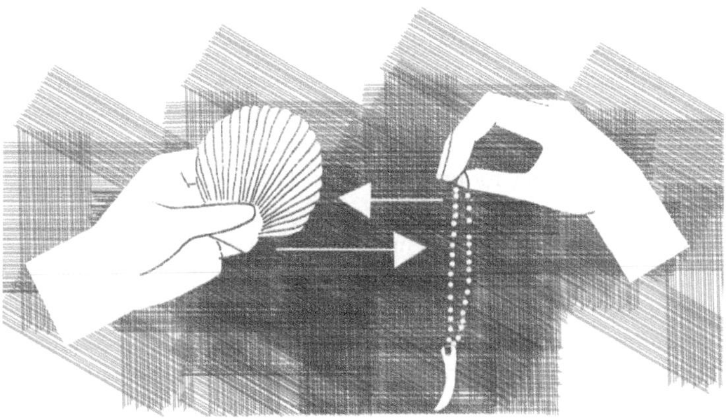

Figure A.4b Instance of classical exchange (close-up).

The world would have to await the arrival of other classes of exchange capable of further loosening these invariance requirements on these properties of tenure, and with it, the magnitude or volume of image of value – and which in turn would then allow for the differentiation of the new economic properties of maturity and interest rate. For in the Paleolithic era classical exchange was the only available class of exchange, and such class of exchange did not and does not allow that any economic properties of the object other than its orientation can change in the course of its motion from one to another place in space.

For this reason, we must also observe that a class of exchange whose rigid motions congruently preserve the image of value of the object over the tenure of the exchange (the latter of which, again, is always defined as immediate settlement) will necessarily preclude the admittance of any transactions involving debt and/or equity objects, not to mention credit derivatives or any other synthetic financial objects. For all early instances of exchange consisted of a single class of transformations: this class of transformations consists of the rigid motions of congruence; and economic congruence is original to classical exchange.

iii To be sure, then, there is nothing exclusively 'classical,' per se, about classical exchange. We would label it 'normal' or 'ordinary' or 'school' exchange instead, were it not but for the risk of perpetuating a naïve presumption taught in schools of leftist political economy that this class of exchange is most ordinary and normal. Whether it *is* in fact, as it is so often thought, the most blue-collar, pedestrian, or 'real' of the classes of exchange is a question whose answer is at best uninteresting for the purposes of satisfying our objectives herein. We would say 'it certainly is the oldest of the classes of exchange' though this assertion will no doubt quickly become problematic, were a good anthropological account of exchange to broaden the notion of exchange sufficiently enough. In some sense it is the most obvious, and today still likely the most widely known of the subclasses from the general class of automorphisms of exchange – even if we will not say that it is indefatigably the most material' which, based on our examinations of synthetic finance, we now know would be an unwarranted claim. And while there is no further data we should or could cite to substantiate our assertion of the ongoing contemporary ubiquity of classical exchange, e.g., of the total number of congruent transformations in the last fiscal year, of its total market cap, and so on, its continued persistence today is just so obvious.

The important question here is: if the motions of congruence do not exhaust the total motions available as a class of exchange, what are the other classes of exchange, what are their motions, and what are their invariance requirements? This perhaps is merely an uncontroversial manner of observing that symmetry has more guises than simply that of congruence. And this in turn is merely a matter of observing that there are different structures to different spaces of exchange, which then determine the amount and kind of symmetry marking any given economic object as it is exchanged for its image of value as money.

For this reason, we must inquire further into the quantity and quality of symmetry marking these other classes of exchange. This is a present and future concern for speculative materialism.

Appendix 3 – Generic finance

i. In Appendix 2 we alerted our reader to an existing isomorphism between the congruent motions of classical geometric transformations and the congruent motions of classical exchange. Each group of motions, while of different objectival registers, share in common a certain conception of symmetry –and with it the ontology that follows: the property of orientation of the object is allowed to vary, i.e., orientation is not invariant to change; but an otherwise rigid set of invariance requirements pre-restrict the other properties of the object as it moves into its image, and from one to another place in space.

The reason for this mutual conflation of symmetry with congruence is due to a shared conception of space as flat and not curved, and the distance between all points and lines as fixed, regular, and everywhere the same. It is worth noting that classical geometry did not originally call this space 'Euclidean,' insofar as all space – ambient, Cartesian-coordinated, and absolute – *was* Euclidean; it was simply understood as 'space,' generally and as such. Only with the 19th century advent of non-Euclidean spaces of transformation did this conception of space retroactively come to be regarded as specialized, and was then subsequently labeled 'Euclidean,' in order to now delineate the extrinsically defined subspace metrics of Euclidean space from those of the intrinsically defined metrics of non-Euclidean spaces.

We will follow suit by now formally observing that the space of exchange of classical exchange is 'Euclidean,' in order to delineate the subspace metrics of Euclidean markets from the intrinsically defined non-Euclidean markets of synthetic finance.

The question that arises is, what *is* the structure to the space of exchange of finance? And insofar as we know that there are not one but two classes of financial exchange – generic and synthetic – let us apply this question to each of their respective classes of transformations.

ii. To begin with we observed that in classical geometric transformations any two figures are congruent, and therefore belong to the same equivalence class, if their geometric properties can be made to coincide with themselves in every respect. The method devised by classical geometry for establishing whether this is the case, as we saw, is to loosen the invariance requirement on orientation, and to move one of the figures from its place in space until now it is placed on top of the space occupied by the other figure (Figure A.5). And if, when the

Figure A.5 Transformation of an object into its image.

figure is transformed into its image, all properties except the orientation of the figure remain invariant to this change, we know and say that the two figures are congruent, commensurable, equivalent – i.e., *symmetrical*.

However, it turns out that to assert that the rigid motions of congruence are the *only* symmetry transformations possible for geometric figures is not so much always wrong as that it is only sometimes true. We know that this is the case, because already classical geometry begins to permit that some properties of different equivalence classes can be combined by dropping the invariance requirement on area (in 2-dimensions) or volume (in 3-dimensions).

How so? While preserving its conception of the space of transformation as flat and not curved, classical geometry now loosens the requirement that lengths of sides must be the exact same within a given equivalence class, and therein begins to allow for *proportional ratios*: this means that what was previously an invariance requirement on the lengths of line segments of geometric figures is dropped, so that now its sides are free to expand or contract over the course of its transformation; and as a result, along with it, and in proportional ratios, the area/volume of the figure is free to grow or shrink (Figure A.6). However, all other properties of the figure must remain invariant to change: classical geometry continues to require that the figure's shape, its values of angles, its separation into an inside and outside region, and so on will all remain unchanged under the motion of its transformation – but now no longer its lengths of sides, and consequently no longer its area/volume.

So on the one hand, we see that this is the differentiation of a secondary class of motions. And we see that they are *derived* from congruent motions, the latter

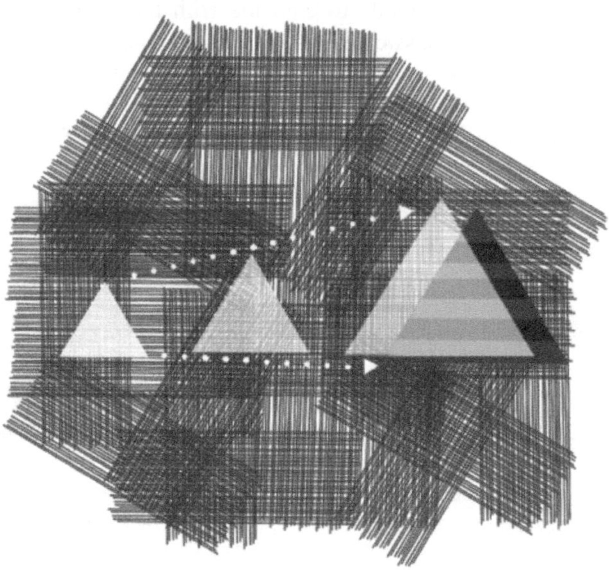

Figure A.6 Similarity transformation.

of which are apparently a *historically* more original class of geometric motions. And while this new permitted transformation cannot be said to 'congruently' preserve all geometric properties of the figure when it moves from one to another place and into its image, these motions nonetheless do preserve a 'similar' image. For this reason, classical geometry labels the motions that comprise this equivalence class 'similarity motions': such class of motions does not congruently preserve as invariant *all* geometric properties of the figure, but it does keep them 'similar' enough.

On the other hand, we have observed that the transformation of a geometric figure by manner of similarity motions will not only not preserve the orientation of the figure (as already occurs with congruent motions), but now also will not preserve the figure's lengths of line segments – and consequently will not preserve the volume of the geometric figure when transformed into its image (Figure A.6). Because this means that all figures that are *similar* to themselves now comprise an equivalence class of figures in their own right – a similarity class of geometric figures – we see that in this new class of transformations, all rectangles that are either congruent *or* similar are now equivalent, and also all circles that are either congruent *or* similar are now equivalent, insofar as volume is no longer an invariant geometric property. Or what is to say the same thing: in similarity geometry there is no material distinction made between different proportions so long as their ratios are preserved, for any figure whose volume will grow or shrink as it moves into its image is still regarded as symmetrical with that image, so long as its other geometric properties remain unchanged (Figure A.7).

Consequently, while similarity appears *historically* derived from and in some sense ostensibly predicated on congruence, we also see that similarity already contains the class of congruence transformations within itself –but not vice versa– and that therefore similarity is both a larger class of transformations, and

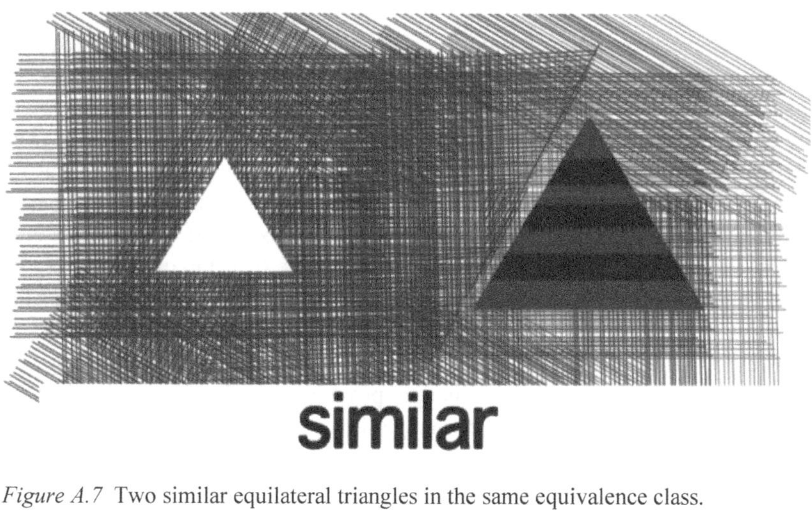

Figure A.7 Two similar equilateral triangles in the same equivalence class.

is therefore said to *ontologically* have more symmetry than the class of congruent transformations from which it appears historically, ostensibly, and empirically derived.

iii. In classical exchange, we know that two economic objects are congruent if their different material properties can be made to coincide with their image of value in every respect. The original method devised by non-money-mediated versions of classical exchange (as we saw in Appendix 2) for achieving commensurability between different quantities of qualitatively distinct objects was to establish whether they belonged to the same equivalence class of objects; and that this was accomplished by moving one or more objects from their place in space, until their images of value were made to coincide with the images of value of the other object or sets of objects (Figures A.4a and A.4b).

We have observed, with Heichelheim, the practical problems associated with this method of exchange. We also observed the subtle but radical ontological shift accompanying the advent of money-mediated classical exchange as an attempt to resolve such problems. For now, if, when the object is transformed into its image of value as money, all properties except the orientation of the object remain invariant to change, we know and say that the object and its image of value are congruent, commensurable, equivalent – i.e., *symmetrical.*

However, once again it turns out that to assert that the rigid motions of congruence are the *only* symmetry transformation possible – this time for economic objects transformed in space – is not so much always wrong as that it is only sometimes true. We know that this is the case, because from out of classical exchange we see the differentiation of another class of exchange, which begins to permit non-congruent transformations of an object into its image of value as money, insofar as it loosens the invariance requirement placed by classical exchange on the lengths of tenure of the exchange, and relatedly its volume of the image of value.

How so? Any example of traditional debt or equity objects would equally well illustrate that this is the case. However, let us simply recall that in the course of his discussion of the earliest money-mediated exchanges in the Paleolithic era, Heichelheim stresses that '[a]ll forms of money [used]… differ from the forms of money which we use today, because they could not be lent out for interest.'[7] In other words, Heichelheim is observing that Paleolithic exchange, which is apparently the historically first of all acts of exchange, was always only classical exchange insofar as the volume of the image of value of the object was not allowed to grow or shrink over the tenure of the exchange (and tenure, again, as we have noted, was always defined as immediately settlement).

However, while preserving its conception of the space of transformation as flat and not curved, classical exchange progressively begins to loosen the requirement that the tenure of the exchange, i.e., its temporal length, must be an immediate settlement, and it therein also begins to allow for proportional ratios between the object and its image of value.

Heichelheim relays this differentiation of a new class of exchange – he calls it 'money lending' – albeit first only 'as an exception' to classical exchange. At any rate, it signals the birth of generic finance, which would proceed to progressively differentiate into debt and equity markets, that is to say stock, real estate markets, futures, and options markets (equity), and bond and mortgage markets (debt) – with all of their indices and benchmarks and respective metricizations.

To begin this: the most ancient forms of money which were lent out on interest were 'food money.' If we make use of etymology and of ethnological parallels, we find that this type of money was known to the original Indo-Germanic, Semito-Hamitic, Ural-Altaic, and Sumerian nations, and we are led back, in this way, to the period near 5000 BC if not earlier. Dates, olives, figs, nuts, or seeds of grain were probably lent out, even as early as these periods, to serfs, poorer farmers, and dependents, to be sown and planted, and naturally an increased portion of the harvest had to be returned in kind. Economically, this has to be considered a new characteristic of this money, supplementing its purposes as a means of exchange and valuation.[8]

The radical ontological development occurring within the general class of exchange (that is classical exchange) here is evident. The invariance requirement on tenure as immediate settlement is dropped, so that now different terms to maturity of different exchanges are allowed to expand out further into time; and as a result, along with it, the volume of the image of value of the object is free to grow (or shrink, on occurrence of some credit event) – but always still in proportional ratio to its cash flow, or yield (Figure A.8). However, all other properties of the object continue to remain invariant to change: this new class of exchange imports from classical exchange now into its own invariance requirements the congruence of the object's general shape, its collinearity of risk and ownership,

Figure A.8 Instance of generic finance.

its separation into an inside and outside region to the exchange, and so on, therein ensuring that all such economic properties will continue to remain unchanged under this new class of motions to exchange.

And yet it is interesting to also observe the actualization of a new set of economic properties which did not exist 'in' or otherwise adhere 'to' the classical object: for instance, as the term to maturity is lengthened (or what is to say the same thing – as the invariance requirement on tenure is loosened from and now allowed to be defined as other than simply immediate settlement), and the object's volume of the image of value is allowed to fluctuate, the new property of 'rate of yield' or 'interest rate' is born: interest, then, is here a newly differentiated spatial property of a generic financial asset, but was never a property of the classical object; and 'interest rate,' i.e., as in the 'rate of yield,' is another new temporal property that now supervenes on the object's volume of the image of value. To cite another example, 'risk,' which may have always already been a generalized and virtual property to any prior classical exchange (e.g., how do I know that the 20 yards of linen I receive in exchange for my one chicken will not prove a poor quality of cloth? Or that the one chicken I receive in exchange for my 20 yards of linen will not be diseased?), now becomes actual, more palpable, pertinent, and capable of augmenting with time. In fact, entirely different kinds of risks now begin to differentiate themselves as a property of the generic financial asset: now there is 'default risk' in addition to simply 'fraud risk' or 'quality risk,' e.g., as had been the case with a diseased chicken or poor quality of cloth, and so on, in a classical exchange.

For this reason, we see that the repetition of the classical object by generic finance involves the loosening of some of the former's invariance requirements, but that it also results in the differentiation of new economic properties concomitant with this new class of exchange.

On the one hand, we see that this is the differentiation of a secondary class of exchange; and that its motions appear *derived* from the congruent motions of classical exchange, the latter of which comprise the motions of a seemingly more *historically* original class of exchange. And while this new permitted class of motions does not congruently preserve all economic properties of the figure when it moves into its image of value, its transformations nonetheless do preserve a 'similar' economic object. Indeed, in a generic financial transaction the economic object will never change its general shape as it moves into its image – which, for instance as we have seen, *does* happen in cash and synthetic securitization, credit derivatives, and other synthetic acts of exchange. However, the volume of the image of value of a generic financial asset, e.g., of a bond, is now free to fluctuate over its maturity of 30-days, one-year, ten-years, and so on. And for this reason, we see that the class of motions that is generic finance no longer preserves as invariant all classical economic properties of the object as it is transformed in the course of its exchange, and yet does keep them 'similar' enough.

And so on the other hand, we have also observed that the transformation of an economic object by manner of generic financial exchange will not only not preserve the orientation of the object (an historical invention already boasted by classical exchange), but now will also not preserve the tenure of the exchange as immediate settlement, and relatedly, will not preserve the image of value of the economic object when it is so transformed by the exchange (Figure A.8). This means that there is no longer an invariance requirement on the volume of the image of value of the object over the tenure of a generic financial exchange. Or what is to say the same thing, generic finance makes no distinction made between different proportions so long as the ratios are preserved, insofar as an object whose volume will grow or shrink as it moves into its image is still regarded as symmetrical with that image – were this not the case, there would be no symmetry, which means no price would be arrived at, and no exchange would occur.

For this reason, we see that while generic finance is often regarded as *historically* derived from and in some sense ostensibly predicated on classical exchange, it is also the case that generic finance already contains classical exchange within itself – but not vice versa – and that therefore generic finance is both a larger class of transformations, and *ontologically* has 'more symmetry' than classical exchange.

Let us now consider synthetic finance, which progressively differentiates itself from out of generic finance.

Appendix 4 – Synthetic finance

i. In the course of our discussion of the differentiation of similarity from out of congruence, we became increasingly aware that we were observing the progressive differentiation of an ontologically more fundamental class of transformations from out of a less fundamental class, but that the less fundamental class appears historically prior. We know that there is a quantitative increase of symmetry marking this new, differentiated class of similarity transformations, since it involves the preservation of all of the same geometric properties preserved by congruence, while yet loosening the invariance requirement on length, so that when the figure is reoriented into its image, subsequently a proportional magnification or diminution of the volume of the image of the figure results. For this reason, different sizes of the same geometric figures are symmetrical nonetheless, inasmuch as they belong to the same equivalence class of similarity transformations.

Our reader will have realized at this point that because we have allowed the logic and conceptual resources of symmetry to bathe our own study of the ontology of exchange, we have been able to herein observe the occurrence of a likewise phenomenon in the register of economic exchange. We considered the differentiation of generic financial exchange from out of classical exchange, and became increasingly aware that here too we were observing the progressive differentiation of an ontologically more fundamental class of economic transformations from out of a less fundamental class, but that once more this less fundamental class appears historically prior. We know that there is a quantitative increase of symmetry marking this new, differentiated class of exchange, with all of its objects and new economic properties (e.g., of rate of interest, default risk, etc.) that actualize themselves and proliferate en masse, since the exchange of such objects involves the preservation of all of the same economic properties preserved by classical exchange – except, of course, and importantly, that by loosening the invariance requirement on the property of tenure as immediate settlement, when the object is reoriented into its image of value as money, subsequently a proportional magnification or diminution of the volume of its image of value as money results.

This comprises the ontological process of generic finance, it is the ontological consistency of any generic financial exchange, it is the ontological commonality shared by all generic financial assets – it marks the ontology of the *generic asset*, as such. Whether considering *generic debt*, i.e., all fixed income instruments, such as bonds, bills, notes, commercial paper, mortgages, and so on; or whether *generic equity*, such as stocks, insurance, real estate, or options: in all such acts of generic financial exchange, as the asset is reoriented into its image of value as money, we see that the invariance requirement placed by classical exchange on the property of tenure is loosened, so that now the term to maturity of the exchange is allowed to extend out into time, which means that settlement is no longer defined as immediate; and with it, the volume of the image of value as money begins to grown or shrink, and the new properties of 'rate of interest' and 'default risk' differentiate from out of their prior classical incarnations of simple 'one-time yield' (at the point of sale, an immediate settlement) and general 'counterparty risk.' However, once again, all other such economic properties of the object that are invariant under a classical exchange continue to remain invariant in generic finance.

We have only been able to materially evaluate this ostensibly historically secondary but ontologically more original class of exchange because we have examined the quantity of symmetry marking each of these two respective equivalence classes of exchange. We have already observed in Appendix 1 that the study of invariance under conditions of transformation was initially a group-theoretic concept applied to the study of the ontology of geometric spaces. For this reason, in future work we must revisit two mathematical group theorists par excellence, Evariste Galois and Felix Klein, for a more technical group-theoretic exposition of the concept of symmetry. However, even here it is interesting to pursue this isomorphism between the symmetry of geometric transformations and economic transformations yet further still.

This we now do with synthetic finance.

ii. Similarity does affect the figure, but really not all that much.

Under a similarity transformation, though the figure's lengths of sides and volume may change, the values of its angles are still preserved, any parallel lines will remain parallel, and all other properties known to classical geometry continue to remain rigid, congruent, and otherwise unchanged when that figure is reoriented into its image in space. However, under topological transformations these properties are no longer invariant.

For example, topological transformations do not preserve the values of angles, parallel lines do not remain parallel, and as well, many other classical geometric properties of the figure may undergo fairly radical changes. For this reason, we can see that whereas a similarity transformation will not alter the basic material shape of the figure 'too much' (i.e., it remains 'similar' enough), this is no longer the case in topology. For while in a similarity transformation the volume of the figure may grow or shrink, its exact shape will always be preserved – e.g., a triangle will still remain a triangle, a square a square, a circle a circle, and so on. However, a topological transformation is a thoroughly de-differentiating and re-differentiating process. It may change a circle into either an ellipse, a hyperbola, or a parabola, and vice versa (Figures A.9a and A.9b);

Figure A.9a Topological transformation.

Figure A.9b Topological transformation.

therefore any conic sections (hyperbola, parabola, ellipse, circle) are ontologically indistinguishable in topology – or what is to say the same thing, under the force of topological transformations all conic sections are able to symmetrically transform into their image, inasmuch as they belong to the same equivalence class. Or to take another example, any two lines under topological transformation can intersect, which means that parallel lines need not remain parallel; a square could become a triangle, or metamorphose into any other kind of figure, and vice versa (Figure A.10); or a triangle could open up and stretch its sides out to infinity (Figure A.11); and so on. For this reason, in topology many varieties of different types of geometric figures belong to the same equivalence class.

In this respect, we see and say that there need be no one-to-one correspondence between the points and lines of a given geometric figure when it is transformed into its image. And for this same reason, we will observe that the structure to the space of topological transformations is no longer the familiar Euclidean coordinates of classical geometric transformations, whether of congruence or similarity: it is clearly not flat and zero-curvatured, and the distances between its points and lines are not everywhere the same, as in Euclidean geometric space. Rather its space, or 'domain of action,' is now non-Euclidean, i.e., it is topological, it is curved, its surface is a space unto itself.

There are two points to immediately apply towards the development of our ongoing examination of the ontology of exchange.

Figure A.10 Topological transformation.

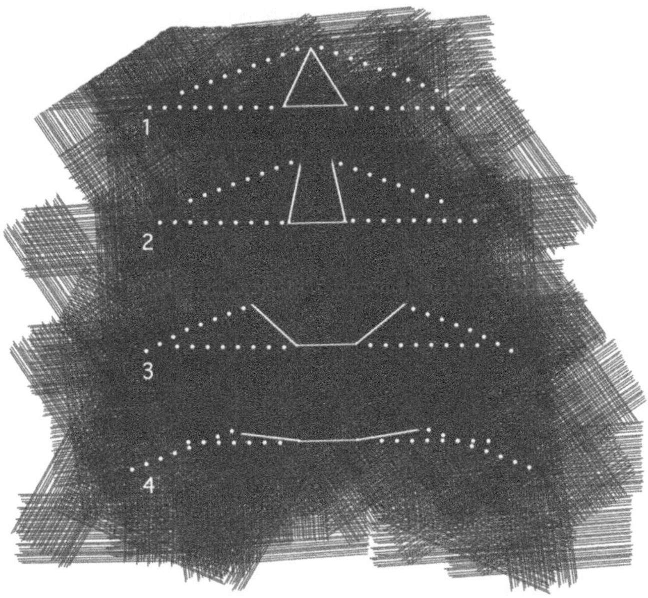

Figure A.11 Topological transformation.

First, it is not unimportant to recall here that our own case study of credit derivatives independently stumbled upon the observation that the differentiation of synthetic finance signals a quantitative increase in symmetry over the other two historically prior classes of exchange of classical exchange and generic finance, insofar as many of their invariance requirements are simply dropped from the synthetic exchange. And importantly, when this happens, we see that an entirely new and unique set of economic properties differentiate themselves, and which were not actual in the other two classes of exchange.

So for example:

Case Study Notes 1–3

In Notes 1–2 we observed that already even in the relatively simple single-name CDS and single-name TRS there is no required collinearity of risk and physical exposure – which notably *is* an invariance requirement in the generic financial exchange of an insurance contract, i.e., wherein one cannot exchange the risk of an object to whose physicality they are originally unexposed or otherwise unrelated. And of course in all other generic financial assets, risk and cash flow are properties that are absolutely collinear with the materiality of the asset, as such (e.g., if a bond is purchased, its risk and cash flow remain attached to the asset).

In Note 3 we furthered examined the loosened invariance requirements marking the exchange of single-name synthetic assets by itemizing a brief list of collinearities whose invariance is required in classical exchange and generic finance, but which are now no longer preserved, namely: (a) not only is there is no invariance requirement on *collinearity of risk and exposure*, e.g., no party to the synthetically replicated risk and cash flow is required to own or otherwise hold original exposure in the referent; (b) but there is now no invariance requirement on *collinearity of tenure*, e.g., the referent obligation can have a different maturity than the synthetically replicated asset; (c) there is now no invariance requirement on *collinearity of notional value*, e.g., the referent may have a different notional value than the synthetically replicated asset; and (d) there is now no invariance requirement on *collinearity 'in-kind,'* e.g., the referent can be any number of different species of financial assets, but which the synthetic asset changes 'in kind' in the process of its replication. So for instance, while we provided the example of a senior secured generic bond vs. a synthetically replicated senior unsecured generic bond, we could have chosen any number of examples to illustrate the profound metamorphosis of the asset in the course of its synthetic replication.

Case Study Notes 4–5

If Notes 1–3 directed us towards the indubitable observation of the hyperfungibility and increased symmetry marking single-name synthetic assets, in Note 4 we observed that this allows for the ready de-differentiation and re-differentiation of synthetically replicated risks and cash flows through the pooling and tranching process of structured finance.

What did we see? We saw that the combination of loosening the aforementioned invariance requirements on such collinearities with now the addition of the technology of structured finance results in the progressive differentiation, or a birth to actuality, of new and unique economic properties specific to multi-name synthetically structured assets: we saw, for instance, the creation of the new properties of 'levels of subordination,' 'attachment points,' 'detachment points,' 'credit enhancement,' and 'natural leverage' – and this is merely the beginning of the new properties that a more thorough exposition of either generically structured or synthetically structured finance would reveal.

In short, then, we observed that the progressive differentiation of synthetic finance involves – quite paradoxically – the quantitative metricization of more economic properties, while yet the process of synthetic exchange involves quantitatively more symmetry. We observed that these properties are organically created, and often by way of a synthetic exchange alone – and at that, are organically created, no less, by manner of loosening one or more invariance requirements present in the historically prior but ontologically less original classes of exchange. And that this means there is more symmetry marking this class of economic transformations, or exchange.

In this respect, in Note 4 our consideration of the creative differentiation that is the process of pooling and tranching endemic to structured finance paved the conceptual foundations for our examination of the synthetic vehicle of credit linked notes in Note 5. Here, then, in Note 5, we saw that, on the one hand, the use of CLNs involve the effective creation of a generic financial asset – a generic financial exchange between the obligor qua CLN issuer and the lender qua CLN investor – *within and through* a synthetic exchange; and that this equates to an organic derivation of a new generic asset from out of a synthetic asset, but whose value is now linked to the value of the synthetic asset: this means that the traditional financial process which defines 'the derivative' as 'an asset whose value is derived from a generic referent asset' has effectively been reversed; for now we derive the value of a generic referent asset (the CLN) from the synthetic. And so, on the other hand, we saw that this means that the CLN investors, who have prefunded protection payments to the CLN issuer, have acquired very real, material, vested interests in the financial wellbeing of the CLN issuer, as well as the continued financial viability of the synthetic portfolio, whose value is the referent to which the value of the notes they hold are linked.

Case Study Notes 6–7

A continuation of the thoughts developed in Notes 4–5 led us to discuss, in Note 6, the technology of a structured investment vehicle (SIV). The most significant observation herein was that by issuing CLNs linked to itself, the SIV creates itself as an asset-backed security.

How can we fail to observe the profound material significance – as outlined in Notes 1–6 – of the progressive differentiation of a new class of exchange that at once reveals the portable hyperfungibility of the economic properties constitutive of an asset by way of a technology that antedates the very concept of private property?

For this reason, in Note 7 (and our reader is here encouraged to reread Note 7 and our 'Ending with a Modest Proposal' at this time) we began to speculate about the construction of a universal synthetic CDO, the material composition of whose reference portfolio was a co-equal split between (i) gross global product and (ii) an individual's annual taxable income. This would simultaneously leverage everyone on top of everyone, and tether each individual reference portfolio to a combination of collective and individual wealth. If everywhere everyone was an originator of their own synthetic CDO composed in the manner outlined and illustrated in our modest proposal, but also every person was a CLN investor of every other synthetic CDO everywhere, the following question arises: *Is it the historical-materialist significance of the progressive differentiation of synthetically structured finance precisely that for the first time in the history of humanity, what is the most equitable is also now the most profitable?* This is a remarkable prospect to indulge, and indeed is either only absolutely crazy, or absolutely crazy and also true.

Second, then, there is also a major point here that is a Deleuzian point, or perhaps rather a speculative materialist point, to underscore. It is a point about a new difference produced through repetition: we have seen that the object is repeated through the process of its synthetic replication, but through its very repetition a new difference is produced. Here then, we must realize that we are now capable of synthetically creating the organic – and if the organic *is* capital, it has been created by way of exchange qua circulation, not simply, exclusively, or even any longer by way of production.

Of course, let us note that all of our abovementioned observations are predicated on the quantitatively increased symmetry marking synthetic exchange; but then again, such increased symmetry is predicated on the hyperfungibility of risk and cash flow, i.e., their abilities to be plastically deployed and redeployed, or created and destroyed willy-nilly; which means that such symmetry is not simply quantitatively increased, but also *qualitatively* different in kind. Let us not overlook the crucial fact that none of the progressively loosened invariance requirements marking synthetic exchange would occur were it not but for the fact that risk and cash flow are *extensive* properties of the exchange, whose plasticity ensures their fungible creation, destruction, extraction, injection, distribution, and redistribution alike.

For this reason, when we are seeing and saying that there is no one-to-one correspondence between the properties of given synthetic assets when transformed into their images of value in space, we should be aware that we are observing that the space of synthetic finance is no longer the familiar economic space of either classical exchange or generic finance – i.e., it is clearly not the flat and zero-curvatured Euclidean space familiar to classical and neoclassical economics. Rather, its space, or 'domain of action,' is non-Euclidean: it is topological, its surface is a space unto itself. Moreover, it is becoming increasingly topological, which is to say that *capital in its synthetic incarnation is regressively differentiating to topology.*

Further examination of the structure to the space of synthetic finance is therefore a future task for speculative materialism. For this reason we now turn our attention, in closing, to the study of multiplicities, or the dynamical material structures of the assets and markets they populate.

Appendix 5 – Markets as multiplicities

i. We have discovered an isomorphism between geometry and exchange, insofar as both fields maintain certain invariance requirements on the properties of the objects under transformation in space.

We observed that classical geometry from the beginning already incorporates a very specialized conception of invariance into its concept of symmetry – defined, strictly speaking, as congruence; and we know that this was due to its presumption about the structure to the space of transformation. If a figure is said to be congruent – and therefore symmetrical – when reoriented into its image, but now in a different place in space, this can only be due to the fact that the structure to the space of transformation is rigid, flat, zero-curvatured, and the distance between all points and lines are homogeneous and everywhere the same: in short, this space is Euclidean. And likewise, even if the invariance requirement on lengths of sides is loosened, so that the volume of the figure is allowed to grow and shrink over the course of its transformation, 'similarly' scaled copies of the figure will still be produced, and all other properties of the figure will continue to remain unchanged: in short, this space too is Euclidean. Things may then be said to change, or vary, under this kind of transformation;

but it is an invariable form of variation, an empty kind of change; things may change, but really not all that much.

It was this existing isomorphism between geometrical transformations and the transformations of exchange that allowed us to observe that congruence is to classical exchange what similarity is to generic finance – and that the structure to these spaces of exchange are the flat and zero-curvatured Euclidean space of their transformation. So too, our speculative materialist question going forward is that if topology is to synthetic finance, *what more can synthetic finance do*? This is a question about the future development of finance as a class of exchange.

In the course of our examination of the ontology of exchange, we have begun to realize that so much depends on what is the structure to a space of exchange.

Is our conception of the space of exchange homogeneous? Is there a single, flat, ambient space, always and only that comprises the space of exchange? Is the structure to economic space a zero-curvatured three-dimensional surface, on which diverse sets of commodities, with all their variant and invariant economic properties walk about, conversing with one another? Or are there different spaces to exchange – both a flat and zero-curvatured space, but also one or more uneven and curved surfaces that are spaces unto themselves? *And if there are different spaces to exchange, does this mean dimension is not an economic invariant?*

The short answer to this question is that we know there must be different structures comprising different spaces of exchange, for otherwise there would never have been possible the acts of exchange belonging to the class of exchange we call synthetic finance. A longer answer involves closer consideration of the meaning of the statement that by 'space of exchange' we simply mean a 'market' and by 'market' we understand that which structures the space of possibilities for the economic properties of the objects populating such spaces – or, for shorthand, by 'market' we mean a 'multiplicity.'

ii. The work of Riemann here is key. We have discussed him already in passing in Essay Three, and we intend to discuss his contributions in more technical fashion, in future work, in more depth. For now, we will merely note that Riemann was instrumental in replacing a Cartesian-coordinated conception geometry, founded on an absolute, fixed, and flat Euclidean space, with an intrinsic geometry of surfaces in n-dimensional space. In the course of this move, Riemann distinguished between the concept of 'space,' by which he meant objective physical space, and 'manifold,' by which he meant mathematical space: in turn, the problem, for Riemann, was to understand *space as a manifold.*

To this we will add that just as there is 'space' qua objective physical space, and 'manifolds' qua mathematical/geometric spaces, so too there are 'multiplicities' qua manifolds of economic spaces that we call markets. A speculative materialist therefore understands that by studying markets we are really studying multiplicities.

When speculative materialism asserts that markets are multiplicities, we should understand the following about the structure to these various n-dimensional spaces of different classes of exchange:

(a) Markets are immanent to material processes, though they are immaterial entities in themselves; they are nomadic spaces that distribute the structure to space itself, rather than sedentary spaces distributed in or on some predefined structure.
(b) The metrical properties of markets are always intrinsically defined; there are no higher supplementary dimensions extrinsically defining its metrics.
(c) Markets are composed of a variable number of dimensions. This means both that dimension is not necessarily always an economic invariant, and that markets are meshed together into a continuum whose metrics are not smooth or consistent.
(d) Markets give structure to the space of exchange; they are presently the domain of action wherein objects are exchanged for money – but one wonders whether this too is merely an invariance requirement? For if the invariant requirements placed on the exchange of any given object – and thus its class of exchange – is determined by the structure to the space of the multiplicity of its market, by modifying the structure of its space, so too do we potentially loosen any given invariance requirement we wish to choose.

For these reasons, the speculative materialist is very motivated to think and create new markets. For markets, and especially markets for the circulation of synthetic assets, structure the space of possibilities for the distribution of risk and cash flow.

Notes

1 For example, J. Maynard Smith and G. Vida (eds.), *Organizational Constraints on the Dynamics of Evolution*, Manchester University Press, 1990; F. Yates *et al.* (eds.), *Self-Organizing Systems: The Emergence of Order*, Plenum Press, 1987. For instance, we see modern neuroscience speak of the self-amplifying fluctuations in synaptic density from an initially undifferentiated and spatially disordered brain, productive of the broken symmetry that results in neurocentral organization. Microbiologists studying the aggregation of slime-mold stress the importance of symmetry-breaking and entrainment for the progressive actualization of a multicellular organism. Embryological research on egg-fertilization emphasizes the organizational work of cleavage patterns, transforming a highly symmetric ooze into differentiated tendons and muscles, blood, brain, and bones. Cosmologists model the expansion-to-cooling phase of our universe to gain insight into the symmetry-breaking bifurcations that allowed for the differentiation of our basic physical forces (at the extreme high temperatures precipitating the birth of our universe, the four forces were yet one). Even geologists studying hydrological patterns are delighted to observe pattern-generating asymmetries of river-formation, as the dynamical flow of water bifurcates, inscribing its sculptures into the face of our Earth.

2 H. Graham Flegg, *From Geometry to Topology*, The English Universities Press, 1974.

3 Fritz Heichelheim, *An Ancient Economic History: From the Palaeolithic Age to the Migrations of the Germanic, Slavic, and Arabic Nations (Volume I)*, A.W. Sijthoff-Leyden, 1965, p. 22.
4 Ibid. p. 53.
5 Ibid. pp. 53–54.
6 Ibid. p. 22. Also see p. 54: 'All forms of money which have been mentioned so far differ from the forms of money which we use today, because they could not be lent out for interest.'
7 Heichelheim p. 54.
8 Ibid. p. 54.

Index

Page numbers in **bold** denote figures.